NINA HERSH

30

MINUTE MARKETING:

101 WAYS
TO WOW CLIENTS,
CUSTOMERS, AND
PATIENTS IN LESS THAN
30 MINUTES

Printed in the United States of America
ISBN: 978-1-936839-08-7

Easy Read Publishers
4000 E. Bristol Street, Suite 3
Elkhart, IN 46514
574-320-2522

Dedication

This book is dedicated to my Grandpa Wing who was the inspiration for my entrepreneurial spirit; my dad & mom, Jack & Joyce Bellows, who always encouraged me to explore and go beyond normal; my children, Tyler, Anya & Pascal who put up with all my crazy ideas and were tolerant even when I was so focused on what I was doing I would forget to pick them up from school (more than once); and to Eldon, my long suffering, loving, always-there-for-me husband. Without him I would never have had the courage to explore my dreams.

To my mastermind team who helped with many of the ideas in this book and is a constant blessing to me and who I'm honored to serve.

To my amazing customers and clients for whom without them none of these ideas would have been tried, true and tested.

And not least – my amazing God who so loved me enough to give me life, a purpose, and salvation.

> [11] For I know the plans I have for you," declares the LORD, "plans to prosper you and not to harm you, plans to give you hope and a future. [12] Then you will call on me and come and pray to me, and I will listen to you. 13 You will seek me and find me when you seek me with all your heart.
>
> *Jeremiah 29: 11 - 13*

Table of Content

Part 4: On Location   35

Part 5: Talking to Customers   43

Part 6: Show Your Gratitude   51

Part 7: Express Yourself   61

Part 9: **Making the Most of Mail** **77**

Part 10: **Going Where the Money Is** **85**

Part 11: **Special Events** **95**

Part 12: Miscellaneous... Life Lessons and Other Stuff 109

SPECIAL BONUS TIP!!!!

Appendix 113

When Nina asked me to write the forward to her book, I knew it was going to be action packed and stuffed with ideas. Everything Nina does, is.

But, I had no idea of the power within the pages of what Nina has created. It completely blew away my expectations with page after page of very specific and tangible things to go do in your business. And yes, I looked at every single one of them and have no doubt they can be executed in under 30 minutes. Wow!

Don't let that 30 minutes thing fool you though, each of the 101 ways to wow could easily stand alone with each one bring significant value to your business, your clients, customers, and patients. Just because you can do it fast doesn't mean it won't last forever and bring you a lot of money.

Before you begin this fast paced adventure of wowing people, I'd like to share with you a few things about your author, Nina Hershberger, a close personal friend of mine and a private client.

There aren't enough words laying around to describe Nina and do her any justice, because she has such extensive background and expertise over marketing, business development, and brand creation that you can't describe what she does, you truly have to see it, hear it, and learn about it firsthand.

You are getting a glimpse into all that she can do and the vast array of strategies Nina has up her sleeve in her arsenal.

If you bring Nina a problem, not only will you get a solution, you'll leave with a better business. If you give Nina an idea, not only will she help you bring it to money, she'll execute on your idea, have a business built around your idea, and marketing in motion before you can finish writing your name on the paper.

I've known Nina for a few years indirectly, and over the past year have had the opportunity to work with her in my Private Coaching Program, and I can tell you, having traveled the country and continuing to do so, I have never run across a person who can take any idea, and opportunity, and challenge in anyone's business and come up with a way to monetize it and/or make it better as reliably as Nina can.

Specific to this book, I happened to be a big proponent of personality marketing, appreciation marketing, and relationship marketing, all slightly different but one in the same, and every one of those are related to WOW Marketing which Nina has done a masterful job of showing, teaching, and providing you with specific and easy to profit from ideas in this book.

Perhaps the thing that has always impressed me the most about Nina is her ability to take an idea and make it come to life. She is an artist of marketing and takes great pride in each and every one of her clients and their businesses. She practices what she preaches with WOW marketing in every aspect of her life.

Now, let's get one thing straight, Nina's made this as easy as possible for you, all that's left is you take each strategy and plugging it into your business. At the end of the day, one thing must happen before anything or anyone else can benefit, that's IMPLEMENTATION.

With Nina's 30 Minute Marketing you're left with bite sized chunks of business growth and success that even the smallest business owner or hoping-to-be-someday-entrepreneur can take action and implement.

This book should become your Marketing encyclopedia to reference and review and constantly go back and pick up another strategy and run with it. Nothing happens until something is implemented. I believe this book will be your catalyst for greater achievements.

Personally, running a multi-million dollar consulting practice and managing dozens of private client businesses, if I were asked what was the one single most significant thing I would attribute my success to?

That answer would be – Relationships.

And in my life, there is not a relationship that I value any more than the one I share with Nina Hershberger. I believe you'll feel the same way by the time you reach the end of this book, now, as long as you've got less than 30 minutes, why not start now, get to work, let's turn this book into profits by Wowing your clients, customers, and patients...go get 'em.

Scott J Manning
www.MillionDollarMethods.com

Scott Manning is a millionaire maker. He takes no incoming phone calls and is not accessible through incoming email. He seldom takes on new clients, charges outside clients $1,000 an hour for individual consulting and has a waiting list for his Private Coaching Program. He is routinely approached regarding ideas and businesses who want to partner with him through his Area Exclusive Marketing Management Program.

Manning walks the walk, by only taking on Clients he will confidently generate at least $250,000 in ongoing royalties from himself from an individual project. He often tells his clients he's interviewing for one of his programs, "with me, you're buying SPEED & CERTAINTY". Some people mistake his confidence, for arrogance but sit in a room with him briefly, get him involved in your business, and you'll soon see, whatever you want to call it, it's well warranted!

Introduction

I'm honored you chose to pick up and read this book. It's no ordinary book. It may never be on the national best seller list, but I guarantee you if you study (and implement) the ideas, tips, stories, and wisdom in these pages it will change your business life. I know that's a bold statement. All I ask if for you to put aside your doubt long enough to use at least 3 of the ideas in your business.

One of the keys of my years in business has been the ability to WOW my customers – and that's basically what this book is all about. It's packed with over 100 tactics, ideas, and strategies to help you WOW your clients, customers, or patients – as well as your business -- successfully.

This material is not to be taken lightly. By learning how to WOW your customers on an on-going basis, you'll be able to:
- Create a customer base that lasts a lifetime,
- Build relationships with your customers, so they stay with you and don't even look at your competition,
- Generate more referrals than you ever thought possible...which will grow your bottom-line without adding to your expenses,
- Create a loyal fan base that will allow you to sell your business down the line, if you so choose (for big bucks!),
- And much more!!!

Look at this book as a buffet of ideas for you to go out and take action on. You're not going to like them all. Some may not even apply to you and your situation. But if you take the time to read them all, chances are even the ideas that don't apply to you will spawn your own ideas. And that's where you'll find your real success!

Now, as you already know, everything you learn in here is for not if you just read this book and put it down. The real results come from taking the ideas, making them your own, and taking action on them. Success in life and business comes from the action you take, not the lessons you learn.

So, read on my friend...and take action on the ideas that suit you best...and go out and get the results you want!

Enjoy and make it happen!

Nina Hershberger

nina@megabucksmarketing.com

Business
Basics

Through the years I've spent in business I've learned one very important truth. The way I run my business IS marketing – it defines who I am and what I do. Everything else builds from that foundation, so it's very important that foundation is solid. This book is a compilation of my own real-world experiences proven successful, as well as the experiences of other smart business owners I have tapped into. Without exception we all know it starts with the basics. If you get the basics wrong, you don't have a successful business.

With that in mind, we'll start at the beginning.

Be the Leader – Your Business Is YOU!

People buy from people. People they know, like, and trust. The advantage small companies have over big dumb companies is that they can add a lot of themselves into the mix.

Your business is *your* business – which means you're the person responsible for leading your customers and your employees (as opposed to the other way around!). That means that whatever I want my business to be, it's up to me to set that example for everyone else.

For example, say in your business that image is important – things have to look just right. Now, if you walk out to greet a customer with a big blob of mustard on your tie, that's not exactly going to deliver your message.

So remember, it's not just what you say as the leader; you have to walk the walk and set an example.

(And maybe, just in case, keep a spare tie in your office drawer.)

2. Do the Right Thing

Lou Holtz is the greatest turnaround coach in the history of college football. He took nearly winless teams to bowl games after he arrived. Lou has three simple questions he asks before he chooses to work with anyone:

1. Can I trust them to do the right thing?
2. Are they committed to doing their best?
3. Do they genuinely care about people?

Me with my friends and mentors, Lou Holtz and Jim Connelly

To see for yourself if the technique works, Coach Holtz suggests putting the method to the test in the following way. Think of two people: one whom you admire and respect and one whom you have a problem with. Answer yes or no to three questions about each person. Can you trust him or her? Is he or she committed to excellence? Does he or she care about you and the organization? With the person you admire and respect, you have clarified why. With the person you have a problem with, you have clarified that you cannot trust the person, he or she is not committed, or he or she does not care.

Find Your Passion!

Joel Bauer was born with spinal meningitis. His mother was told he was going to die and should go home so she wouldn't have to watch him suffer in a hospital incubator. Joel was left in an incubator for two weeks. Doctors gave him an experimental drug that killed 98.2% of all children who took it but...Joel survived.

From then until Joel was seven years old, he just sat in a corner and played with a piece of paper. His mother thought he was the most well-behaved child on earth, but all her friends and family said Joel was retarded, a moron...hopeless.

Joel Bauer – always the entertainer

Fortunately for us, Joel's mother moved him from Philadelphia to upstate New York to remove him from all the negativity. She didn't want to believe Joel was retarded. It was in New York – at age 7 – that he was introduced to magic. Joel failed first, second, and third grade, but all the while he was excelling at and perfecting his magic tricks.

By the time Joel was 13, he was making $30,000 a year doing birthday parties and bar mitzvahs.

By age 15 he was a stage performer on Carnival Cruise Lines, and one year later he became the youngest featured entertainer in the cruising industry.

Later in life Joel used his skills to help huge companies attract the attention of potential customers at some of the largest trade shows in the world. Joel gets paid tens of thousands of dollars to persuade people to the mammoth company's way of thinking, to move potential customers to action, and to help those companies preserve those new relationships with their customers for life.

Today Joel teaches people from all walks of life how to find and live their passion. And once they do, the road to profits are almost guaranteed.

Never Give Up

If it hasn't already happened, trust me – it will. You'll feel like giving up. On your business, on your kids, on your friends, on your spouse, on your job, and maybe even on yourself. The list of things to give up on is endless. Winston Churchill is credited for saying, "Never, never, never give up". I echo that statement. And I'm going to give you 12 reasons why:

- As long as you're alive, anything is possible.
- Joel Bauer.
- Michael Jordan.
- Lance Armstrong.
- Someone with fewer skills than you has done it, so you can do it also.
- There are billions of people worse off than you who would love to trade places.
- When you win, you can give back. It is your God-given obligation to give back and give forward. You're living in the richest country in the world. How dare you even think of giving up?
- There is no such thing as getting rich quick. If you see someone who seems to have the Midas touch or who something happened to very quickly, I'll show you someone who failed and failed and failed until he/she finally got it right. They never gave up.
- Life is not a bowl of cherries, but lemonade sure tastes good.
- Helen Keller.
- You are soooo close.
- Because I said so.

Success comes to those who never give up, keep pushing forward, fail fast, pick themselves up, and stay in the game. Consistency over time minus emotion = success.

Monitor Your Employees

There's a saying: "inspect what you expect." That means we inspect what our employees are doing, whether it's a routine job or something a little more complicated, to make sure what they do meet our expectations. Because if it meets the owner's expectations, it will meet the customers' expectations, too.

And on the other hand, if we don't inspect...how will we even know what we're getting? Chances are we won't until a customer doesn't get what he expects – and by then, it will be too late.
President Reagan used to say "trust but verify." I believe that saying will serve you well in life.

Walk the Halls
(Story from John Cohoat)

Even now, 20-plus years later, people still remember me from when I was a chief executive at a hospital. And what they remember is me walking the halls.

I would go *everywhere* in that hospital -all the floors, the clinical departments, even the maintenance areas. I'd talk to the nurses at their stations and the patients in their rooms. And by knowing every corner of that hospital, I had a deeper understanding of what was going on. I could tell if things were working well or not so well, and I could spot problems I don't think I would have noticed otherwise.

When you really, really know and understand your business, you almost instinctively know how to keep it on track. And you only get that kind of understanding by "walking the halls."

In today's world it might mean even going to visit your customers at their places of business. At least once show them how important they are to you. Of course, if you have too many clients or they are spread all over, that might not be feasible, but a quick personal note can go a long way toward getting the same result as "walking the halls." At the very least, visit your most profitable clients and your newest ones.

Remember Your Purpose

A lot of times, we get so busy working in our business that we forget why we're doing what we do in the first place! And, no, don't say it's to make money – nobody goes to your business just because they want to give you money. You're not that special.

Zig Ziglar (Christian motivational speaker and sales expert) used to have a good saying, and we all should try to live by it. "Always give everybody else what they want, and you will have everything that you want." Remember – the only radio station your customers are listening to is WIIFM (What's in it for me?).

Don't Do It All

If I were a chef with my own five-star restaurant, I wouldn't want to spend all my time chopping vegetables or washing pans. It takes a lot of work to run a successful business, but where is the law saying you're supposed to do all of it? Then you delegate some of the lower-tier jobs, you get to be more creative and do the fun stuff you went into business to do in the first place.

The best decision a business owner can make is hiring an associate or - even better in this Internet age - a virtual assistant to take over some of your responsibilities. Figure out how much your time is worth and if you can get someone to do it for less, then delegate.

Formula:

Your annual sales value or gross income in dollars _____

Divided by your actual productive hours working on the business _____

(don't count vacation, or time on busywork, just count actual productive hours that add to your profit).

= What is your hourly potential value? _____

For instance, if your time is worth $150 per hour, is the project you're about to start working on something you should be doing yourself? Now ask yourself, what is the most productive thing I *can* be working on right now?

You'll be surprised. Chances are your clients will get better service, your time will be freed up to produce the high-value profitable things for your business, and you'll have given someone else a job. It's a triple win.

Hire Virtual Help

Let's talk more about hiring a virtual assistant. No, I'm not advocating putting a robot to work. I'm talking about a virtual assistant, also known as a VA. These are different professionals who you can hire online to take care of all kinds of jobs for you, such as research, bookkeeping, copywriting, you name it. Some of them work by the hour, so if you need a list of things done, you can hire an hourly VA and he'll take care of everything for you. Or if you're working on a specific project like a website or a direct mail campaign, you can hire someone for that specific project and call it a day.

Are there risks with hiring a complete stranger you've never even met? Of course. But there is one very important secret to working successfully with a VA:

Don't expect too much too soon.

Start with something simple. If he doesn't perform, you pay his/her fee, say thank you very much, and move on. But if he does something extraordinary, keep her and continue to give her stuff. One person I know has a guy in India who does statistical analysis for her and he's brilliant, so she uses him all the time.

A really great VA is worth a lot to your business. Be sure to have standard operating procedures (SOPs) in place for everything you can. Then your VA will always know how to handle every situation in the manner you want it handled. The more that's in writing, the better.

You can find VAs at Guru.com, Elance.com, oDesk.com, and Scriptlance.com, just to name a few. I wrote an article about hiring VA's. You can read it at **www.MegaBucksMarketing.com/Hire-a-VA**

Channel the Donald

A lot of folks, especially people just starting a business, take anybody and everybody on as a client. Which makes sense when you're starting out. You need volume. But how many of us have had one of those customers who, every time they come into the business, they drag everyone down?

At one time or another, everyone has to deal with a client who's argumentative, too demanding, or simply not easy to get along with.

The most successful business owners have developed a solution.

They fire them.

It's your business, which means you've earned the right to work with who you want to. So let a disruptive customer go, albeit in a very polite, respectful, *non-confrontational* way.

A simple letter that says something like, "Sorry, Mr. Jones, but we just don't seem to be meeting your expectations. We feel you would be much better suited to another company that can better serve your needs, so we will be releasing your account."

You have a business to run – you can't afford to work with people who drain your energy! So let them go and spend your energy on the appreciative customers who help you grow your business.

Raise Your Prices

Before you call me crazy, hear me out.

Who makes more? The expert at the top of the mountain or the newbie at the base camp? Who makes more, a brain surgeon or a general doctor?

We all know the answer to that. The expert – the specialist – of course.

Well, that is who you need to be. The expert.

You probably don't give yourself enough credit for spending the time, money, energy, and years to become an expert in your field. If you're not an expert, then pick another field and become one.

And then charge what you're worth.

Success is between the ears. If you think you can, you can. If you think you can't, you can't.

Decide – and make it happen.

You'll be surprised how many people will pay extra for your expertise! And if they want to nickel and dime you, they're probably not the clients you want to spend all your time on anyway.

You Become What You Think About

Earl Nightingale in his famous recording "The Strangest Secret" summarizes this powerful concept. *You become what you think about.* Think about your rotten customers and you'll have rotten customers. Think about not having money and you'll never attract it. Think about the bad nightly news stories and you'll see pain, suffering, and bad guys around every corner.

But if every day you specifically focus only on the positive, you will reap positive things. Nightingale gives his listeners a 30-day challenge. For 30 days focus only on good thoughts. If a negative thought comes into your mind, stop it immediately.

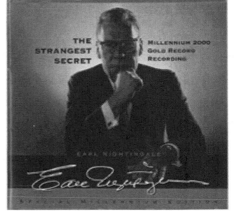

- Quit associating with the whiners and complainers.

- Only spend time with upbeat, positive people.

- Be part of a mastermind of happy business owners who get things done.

- Set specific goals and focus on their attainment.

And you will be surprised how much good will start flowing into your life.

Make Money While You Sleep

One of the biggest fallacies people have bought into is that to make money you have to work hard. There's nothing wrong with hard work, but it's far better to work smart. Leverage your expertise.

Speak in front of a group and have it video taped.

Then have it transcribed. You have now created a home study course.

Get a group of people on a conference call, record it, and have it transcribed. You have now created more products.

Whatever you know more of than the next guy (that does not mean you are the world's #1 expert in that subject – just better than average) there are people who will willingly pay you for that knowledge instead of having to spend time figuring it out for themselves.

Audio CDs and other digital media files are an excellent way to earn extra income, without you having to lift a finger yourself.

And they're easy to create. You don't even have to mail them out. There are fulfillment houses that will take your orders and ship them out.

Your job is to be the expert, to create the products, and to always be marketing!

In general, think about products you can sell online to develop income streams that you don't have to actually do anything to receive. You've only got so much time during the day to earn, so make your off-hours go to work for you, too!

Shop for Success

If you're in the type of business where you regularly interact with movers and shakers, it helps to look (and feel) like you belong. So here's a wardrobe consultant's best kept secret: you don't need a six-figure salary to dress like a CEO. You just need to get creative.

Instead of heading to the mall for your next shopping spree, check out consignment shops in your area, where professionals often resell last year's (still perfectly good) designer clothing at drastically lower prices. Try auction sites like eBay. Or cruise the web for designer closeout sites like Rue la la, Hautelook, and others. There really are dozens of them.

With a little investigating, you can have the wardrobe of a senior executive on a junior exec's budget!

While we're on the subject of wardrobe, hiring a consultant may be the best money you can spend. Hire one to go through your wardrobe (men and women alike) and teach you which colors look best on you, how to mix and match, and how to identify what pieces are missing from your wardrobe. If you don't know any consultants, Kathy Friend is one of the best in the country and can come to you. You can find her at **www.KathyFriend.com.**

*www.KathyFriend.com
Expert wardrobe coach and
personal shopper*

You will then know you'll always look your best and you only have 2/10th of a second to make that lasting first impression.

But whether you're an auto mechanic, a store clerk, or a CEO, being neat and clean is always important. Clients notice appearance.

PART

2

Marketing
101

Before we get into marketing specifics – and there are a lot of them in here – it's important to be sure you have your marketing *systems* down. Get the following few points under control, and you'll be in great shape to get maximum impact from the tips in this book.

Know What Business You're In

You know the business you think you're in? Well, you're not actually in that business.

You're in the marketing business. The marketing of your widget.

Let's say you're a chiropractor. That means you're in the chiropractor business, right?

Wrong! You are a marketer of chiropractic services.

You can always go out and hire another chiropractor. But you can't go out and hire another person to market and grow your business like you can.

This might be THE most important concept in this entire book. If you think of yourself as a marketer – not a technician – your business will change drastically.

Plan your work and work your plan

Planning is important to any business owner. Just as we all know that if you don't know where you're going, you'll definitely get there – nowhere!

There are all types of plans: financial plans, business plans, building plans, etc.

In this tip I want to talk about marketing plans. It's true an entrepreneur wears many hats (actually all the hats), but none is more important than the marketing hat. You can outsource just about everything else. But you can't outsource the marketing.

Coming up with a year's worth of brilliant marketing ideas can be a challenge. The easiest way to get your marketing juices flowing is to create a "marketing calendar" at the beginning of every year.

At **www.MegabucksMarketing.com/Marketing-Calendar** you can read how to pick one zany, offbeat holiday to focus all your marketing around each month. Write the holiday on the calendar and plan everything around it. This helps you think about your advertising specials, newsletter topics, and pictures to use in that month's marketing. The list of possibilities is endless. Starting somewhere makes the job much easier and much more fun.

There's an orthodontist who wants the dentists in his area to send him referrals, so every month, he sends a package to them, and he uses this marketing calendar for inspiration. As you might guess, February is National Chocolate Month, so he sends his list of dentists a jar of chocolates with a little note saying, "Thank you for all your referrals."

By using a marketing calendar, having fun with it, and taking action, he gets about 350 referrals from those dentists every year.

The gift is sent in the mail so it costs very little money, but when you compare that to lead costs that he would've had to have paid to get 350 well qualified referrals, it really is a brilliant strategy!

In my business I figure out who are my top 10 clients for the past year and set up an automated "thank you for your business – I like you" campaign - of course tied into my marketing calendar. They get something from me each and every month and I can't tell you how much that means to people. The easiest way to do this is through Send Out Cards and their automated campaigns. You can find out the details at **www.SendOutCards.com/71230.**

One of the best things about Send Out Cards is their ability to create custom cards.

Here's a card with my husband and I sent last year at thanksgiving time. You can't imagine how many comments I get when I send that card out. And I scheduled it in January for delivery in November. That's what I call putting your plan on auto pilot.

The Gold Is in the List

Your client list is your business's number-one asset.

Know who your clients are. Where do they live, when is their birthday, how many children do they have, what do they read, and what do they do when they're not working?

The gold is in the list. Sliced and diced, niched, and pitched – there is nothing more valuable.

And you won't believe how many business owners don't even have their customer list in any digital form (preferably a database). They don't stay in contact. They don't send them notes. They don't send newsletters. They don't send emails. Nothing. Nada. Zilch.

They just sit back and "pray" that they'll come back and buy.

OK, if it's a really big customer, they may call them once in a while and ask if they have any other business.

But that's no way to treat gold.

Software services like aWeber, Mail Chimp, InfusionSoft, 1Shopping Cart, ACT, Send Pepper, and others help protect that golden list so you can mine it over and over and over.

Dig for Google Gold

You've heard this before: find out what people want and give them what they want. Great. Except the hardest thing is figuring out what it is they want.

But the marketing gods gave us the answer. They gave us Google.

Did you know that every time anyone on the planet goes to the web and Googles something, Google (and every other search engine) keeps track of it? Not only that, they make that info accessible to the rest of us. Meaning we can use *their* research for *our* benefit.

Simply go to Google (the biggest search engine and therefore the one with the most research) and type in "keyword tool." They have their own...so click on it and start finding out what keywords and phrases your customers are searching for to read or buy.

Then, get out there and sell them what they already want!

Create a Google Gauge

Imagine if you had a personal assistant who did nothing but monitor Google for you. You'd hand him a list of search terms, and he'd dutifully type them into Google every day. Anytime something important to your business showed up, he'd email you. Even better, he'd remember which items he'd already sent you, so you only got the new stuff.

Well, that's precisely what Google Alerts does. And it's does it absolutely free of charge!

To sign up for Google Alerts, visit www.Google.com/alerts. Set up an account (if you don't already have a Google account from some other Google product or email, this may take an extra couple of minutes). Once your account is set up, adding alerts is easy. You just have to tell Google a few things:

· The search query you want to track. Example: "personal branding"
· How you want to be notified (email or an RSS feed)
· Whether you want to receive an alert "as-it-happens"(as soon as Google finds a match) or just once a day (if it's a query that triggers a lot of ongoing results, you may want to choose the once-a-day option so you don't end up with a deluge of emails every-other-minute).

So, set up Google Alerts to track your most important items, such as your company name, your key industry terms, and your competitor's names. An important point to remember is that you should use modifiers to winnow down the Google alerts to ones that are relevant to you. For instance, if you just set a Google alert for the word "marketing," you'll be drowning in results. Refining that query to "direct mail marketing" or some other more specific term, and you'll just get what you're interested in.

Always Follow Up

You know how in real estate, everyone says the three most important things you need are location, location, location? Well, I say that in every other business, the three most important things are follow-up, follow-up, follow-up!

Why? Very few sales are ever made with one contact. Yet almost every business will run an ad, and when somebody responds to that ad, if they don't buy, that's when they stop marketing to that person. They let a potential customer who they just spent a whole bunch of money advertising to, walk out the door!

Hardly any sales are made on the first try – it typically takes 8-12 contacts to convert a prospect into a paying customer. The higher the dollar transaction, the more contacts are required. So after spending money to advertise to strangers to get their attention, make sure you have a method and a system to capture their information so they're not strangers anymore.

Of course, that means making sure your employees do what they need to do to capture that information and NOT let a prospect walk out the door or hang up the phone without getting their follow up contact info.

Always Follow Up...Part 2

Follow-up alone will only get you so far if you don't know the secret to successful follow-up. Which is... reminding the client or prospect of what you're following up on in the first place!

In other words, refer to the resume that you sent if you're trying to get a job interview.

If you're trying to get a job and you sent some type of proposal, your follow-up should remind them, "I sent in a proposal on (this date). Just touching base with you to see if you got a chance to look over information because I understand how busy you are."

Whatever you decide to do when it comes to marketing, just make sure you follow-up!!!

Alert the Media

As the famous question goes, if a tree falls in a forest and nobody hears it, does it make a sound? Whatever you think the actual answer is, the marketing response is a definite "NO!"

That means whenever you do anything unusual or different with your business, such as an attention-getting promotion, physically expanding or moving, marking a milestone or partnering with a high-profile associate, you need to make sure somebody "hears the sound." And the best way to do that is a press release.

You may at first think that's a ridiculous notion – who cares what you're up to? But local media especially is always hungry for new stories. They are always under a deadline, so when you hand them a done-for-you story, it solves a problem for them. Keep it informative and educational rather than sounding like an ad if you want a chance of getting it published for free. Depending on what your press release is about, you might even get contacted for a radio or TV interview or get your own story in the newspaper.

Make sure your press release is professional (no typos!) and follows the accepted format (you can find tons of examples online). After it's done, you can submit it online to all sorts of outlets. There are even PR sites that, for a small fee, will distribute it for you! The best one is www.prweb.com.

Numbers Rule

When I say everything, I mean *everything.* Track daily sales, who did the sale, who got the customer in, what advertising media got the customer in, why the customer came in the first place, what kind of work you're doing, who's producing the most and why, who's producing the least and why, where the customer lives, where the customer works, how many miles they traveled to get to you, and what their favorite color is.

Okay, maybe not the last one, but you get the idea...

The reason is that numbers are powerful. If you track them and learn how to read them, they can help you boost your business and make your income more predictable. You don't want a business where all you're getting are the bottom feeders. If you just have a bunch of customers coming in to get your special of the day, or the week or whatever, and that's the only time you see them, you need to change what you're doing. By tracking, you can spot exactly where your strengths are and build on them – and take action with those things that might not be working so well.

Show Some Personality

The deadliest sin in business is being BORING! Small business owners have an advantage over huge corporations. They can be nimble and personable. AND they can add personality to everything they do.

Personality – not perfection – produces profits!

I know, I know...you don't think you're interesting. You don't think anyone wants to know more about you. But you're wrong.

People want to know what you're doing and what you're up to. They want to know about your personal life (not everything – just the fun stuff!) so they can relate to you and feel like you're friends.

They want to know you're an expert (but not perfect).

They want to know what you know.

So, whether you're the life of the party or a homebody, it helps to slip a little of that personality into everything you do. Even if you think you're boring, your customers want to know about that – because it's part of what makes you you.

Remember, people buy from people. They don't want to buy from nameless, faceless corporations – they want to buy from a real, live human being whom they can relate to. They may initially buy from you because of the benefit that they're going to receive, but they'll stick with you because of you.

Still not convinced? How about a cartoon character for personality? I use these custom cartoon characters in everything I do for clients and in my own business. Here's some examples of where I've used them.

Flyer for a trade show for the best dog chews on the planet
www.ScoutandZoes.com

Order form with my cartoon characters

Samples of my famous personality newsletter I create for clients. You can find out more information about them at

www.MegabucksMarketing.com/Newsletter-Templates

Become a Celebrity

Okay, so you're not Brad Pitt or Angelina Jolie. But you don't need to be. You just need to be a star in *your business*.

That means getting out there and being seen. Get your picture taken with people. Talk in front of groups. Put yourself out there.

For example, Debbie Fields became famous as the mom who made cookies. Joan Rivers remade herself from a comedian into a jewelry mogul. Dave Ramsey went from a bankrupt failure to a financial guru.

Trust me. There's something you can become famous for. Forget what your mother taught you. It is okay to leap over your competition. If you don't, someone else will.

This isn't kindergarten, Mildred. You don't have to play nicely in the sandbox.

Choosing a niche is the key here -you can become a celebrity faster when you target one specific audience.

Just don't forget to watch out for the paparazzi!

PART

3

Customer Service

There's no better marketing tool for your business than happy customers because they come back again and again and recommend you to their friends. That's why good, effective marketing starts the minute a prospective customer makes that very first contact with your business.

Meet Their Expectations and Then Exceed Them

Who hasn't been to Disney World and marveled at the smallest detail? If you've ever taken a behind-the-scenes tour, you'll know that EVERTHING to Disney is marketing. And EVERYONE is responsible for that marketing.

Disney doesn't have employees. Disney has cast *members*.

Upbeat music is played as you enter the park in the morning. Calming music is played as you leave in the late afternoon and evening.

No detail is too small, too insignificant, or too unimportant to Disney. Even their cleanliness is marketing.

Take a trip at least once a year to Disney and look through different marketing glasses every time, and then implement what you see in your own business.

Eliminate the Word "No" from Your Vocabulary
(Story from John Cannon)

"No, we don't do that" is never heard around Cannon Automotive. One day a woman came in saying she was told Cannon Automotive could fix some dents in her car.

My first impulse was to say, "No, we're not a body shop."

But because of our culture of never saying "*no*", we checked her car in and put it on the hoist. The dents were there, but there were also quite a few other issues with the car.

We wound up selling her over $3,000 worth of work on that car, and gave a local body shop friend the $2,000 referral job repairing the body damage. And, most importantly, we now have another customer for life (plus a referral business who will try to help us).

In business today, you have to have the "yes" mindset. You have to be flexible and work to serve your customer, or she'll find someone else who will.

Riches are in the Niches

Right now, without you even knowing it, you could be growing your business. There are probably areas where you can be of service to your customers that would fit really well into your business the way it is right now.

The trick is to find them.

What if you had a customer come in with a problem you didn't know how to solve? Instead of sending him away, what if you offered to look into it?

Now suppose you went online and researched what you might be able to do to solve this particular challenge, found a workable solution, and did the work for the customer and he was thrilled? Is it possible that you just found a new source of revenue?

The secret to finding new niches is to always be looking. Keep your eyes and ears open for new opportunities. Go to seminars with the idea of finding new products, new ideas, new joint venture partners, and new ways of doing business.

If it's small, super size it.

If it's big, miniaturize it.

If it's red, make it blue.

If it's a book, make it an audio product.

Always look for new niches. Repurpose what you have. You never know what kind of riches you'll find.

Crack a Smile

Chances are you smile when you greet a customer in person. But what about on the phone? Believe it or not, whether it's a friend, a family member, or even a potential customer, people can actually see you through that phone. Well, not exactly. But they form a picture in their mind, and if you're not smiling, that's a part of the picture.

I don't know why, but I still know that the act of smiling makes you sound and even feel happier. So when that phone rings, no matter what's going on, I stop for a minute, stand up (this gives you more energy on the phone and it's healthy) and smile. I want whoever is on the other end to feel how happy I am to get their call. And people are more likely to buy from a happy person.

Bend Over Backwards

We are all human beings. Mistakes happen. Screw-ups happen. Sooner later, something is going to happen that is going to disappoint one of your customers.

Don't worry about it. Instead, focus on what happens *next.*

I've discovered that if there's an issue with a customer - even if the issue wasn't our fault – I can never go wrong making it right. Taking responsibility and making the customer's comfort and satisfaction a priority, *especially* after something goes wrong, sends a message that they matter to you. It says that your business isn't just about selling a product or service; it's about solving their problem and making their life better.

Send a handwritten apology. It probably will be the first and only one that customer will ever get.

Handle a screw-up gracefully, because often times, this is an opportunity to build some of the strongest customer loyalty you can earn!

PART

On Location

If your business has a physical location like an office or a store, the look, feel, smells, sounds, and even taste of your business all play a role in whether a would-be customer becomes a lifetime fan. Here are a few tips to help you transform your business into a destination your customers love to be.

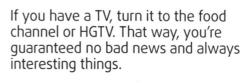

Set the Stage

When somebody walks into a business, they should have the feeling that they're an honored guest. They should feel special. Like you've been expecting their arrival.

Little things like a small refrigerator in the waiting room containing bottles of water for customers. One of the single-cup coffee machines with special coffee. Scented plug-ins to give the waiting area a clean smell (one dentist's wife swears by pineapple cilantro scent by Yankee Candle).Or even a high end coffee maker with special coffee and real cups.

If you have a TV, turn it to the food channel or HGTV. That way, you're guaranteed no bad news and always interesting things.

Fresh-baked cookies, family pictures, and a book of testimonials are all things that can make a person feel at home in your waiting area.

Never to be overlooked is the bathroom. The University of Notre Dame was once on the "best bathrooms in America" list for their main building's bathroom. Clean bathrooms don't happen by accident, and maintaining them certainly is not a fun job, but it's just as much marketing as sending direct mail.

Think out of the box and take advantage of the wall in front of the toilet. Have a framed flyer with that month's special posted at eye level.

Set the Mood

Whether you own a Country Inn and Suites in Northern Indiana or a restaurant featuring home-style cooking in Lancaster, PA, you can "set the mood". Why not have a nice fire roaring in the fireplace (especially on cold winter nights) or a carriage to take the guests through the property?

During Christmas season, have holiday music playing and serve homemade hot cinnamon cider - on the house. Pull out all your grandmother's cookie recipes and start baking up a storm. You could even assemble your own cookbook and give them away or sell them.

Little things, big return. Your clients are welcomed guests – not unwanted pests.

Be Yourself

To me, the heart of marketing is figuring out how my customers can get to know me because if they know me, hopefully they'll like me and be more inclined to buy from me.   So I try to give them some way to relate to me, and I give them a bunch of different options so it ups my chances of forming some kind of connection.

How I do it may not be the way you'll do it, but take an inventory of your skills. Do you love photography? Display photographs you've taken to show your personality, your accomplishments, your hobbies, celebrities you've met, places you've traveled, your family, etc.

When a customer comes in and sees those photos, there's bound to be some area where there's a connection. "Oh, he likes to cook. So do I," or "Oh, she's got kids. I've got grandkids." It encourages people to let down their defenses and opens up the relationship.

Picture This

We've all heard that expression "a picture's worth a thousand words." Well, there's a good reason those words are so well-known.

People think in pictures. If I tell you to think about an elephant, you don't think of the letters e-l-e-p-h-a-n-t, do you? No, you think of a gray mastodon that's as big as your house!

The fact that people think visually is really important when it comes to describing your business. Some people won't understand what you do unless they can see it. So use a lot of pictures on your website, around your office, and in your business literature.

Always Be Marketing

Every aspect of your business is marketing for your business, whether you want it to be or not. Which means that you need to stay on top of *everything*... even the little things.

For example, if you have a Dumpster area and it's messy, that is actually poor marketing.

I know. Your Dumpster area is probably not your primary area of concern when it comes to managing your business. However, if that area turns into a trash pit, you've really got a problem – and it's a marketing problem!

Suddenly, people will start spotting that Dumpster area and think, "He's messy. He's sloppy. He has no follow-through."

And what's even more frustrating is that if you keep your Dumpster area neat and spotless, chances are *no one will ever notice it!*

However, there is still a marketing upside here. If people see that your business is neat and well-organized through and through – from the parking lot to the restroom and everything in between -it feels good to them. And that's good marketing.

That's the kind of stuff that brings people back. And it's the kind of stuff that makes them tell their friends about you.

Send a Message

Even when you aren't physically operating your business, the systems you put in place can still be marketing that business. Take, for example, your voice mail or answering machine. After 20 years, is the best thing you can say still, "I'm not here, can't answer the phone."

Use your voice mail message as a marketing tool. You might say, "We can't come to the phone. We're busy helping another customer with..." and name a product or service you're featuring that month. Or, "After you leave a message with your phone number, check us out on Facebook or check out our website at www dot whatever dot com." Or something funny like, "My dad can't come to the phone at the moment. He's out working really hard to send me to college, so please leave your message, or better yet, just send a really big check."

When you keep it light and fun, it sticks with people -and sometimes they tell their friends to call just to listen to it. Now *that's* marketing!

Use What You've Got
(Story from John Cohoat)

When we owned the Bonnie Doone ice cream shop, our logo had a little girl in it. A lot of our customers would ask who she was. So we decided to have some fun with the concept.

Our daughters were fairly young at the time, so my mother-in-law made them their own kilts, and we dressed the girls up as "Bonnie." They'd visit with customers at the restaurant – as Bonnie, of course - and go to community events, march in parades, and even throw out the first pitch at baseball games!

"Bonnie" put a face to the name of our store and created buzz. Customers would ask her questions about the ice cream she made, have their pictures taken with her, and just "eat up" the whole concept!

You might not have your own Bonnie, but chances are you have something – a pet, a car, even a person – that you can turn into a sort of mascot for your business.

PART

5

Talking to Customers

Unless you do most of your business over the Internet, chances are, in order for your business to be successful; you're going to have to talk to people. And since every word that comes out of your mouth is actually a marketing tool for (or in some cases, against) your business, it helps to follow some guidelines when speaking to prospects, customers, and the public in general.

Here are some tips designed to help transform you into the smooth talker you need to be!

Don't Sell; Present

People go to businesses looking for solutions to a problem – whether that problem is "I'm hungry" or "my car isn't working." So you shouldn't really have to "sell" them anything. All you need to do is present the solutions you offer and explain what you think will work best for them and why.

If you're a chiropractor, you could have the patient's examination results. If you own an auto repair business, you can take customers in to the shop and show them what's not operating properly on their car, or if looking at the actual car would be too difficult, you could show them pictures on a television monitor.

This way, you don't have to "hard sell" customers when you present their problem and possible solutions. After all, that customer came to you with a problem. So it's not about sales really. It's about taking care of the problem. It's about offering the solution.

You build trust by letting customers know that you share their concern and that your goal is to help them find the best solution for their problem instead of simply trying to sell them something.

Be of Benefit

Along those lines, make sure all your marketing materials are all about your customer, not about you. Benefit-oriented copy,in which you're telling your prospects what's in it for them if they use your products or services, is always the most effective. Yes, you need to share your credentials and qualifications, but always do that in terms of how it makes what you're selling more valuable to your customers.

Ask yourself how you can make their life better and what convenience you offer them?

Follow the Script

Have you ever called a business andwhoever answered the phone would say basically whatever popped into their head when asked a question? They had no sales script. No carefully thought out answer to the most commonly asked question. Particularly forgetting to show value when being asked the question "how much is x?"

A lot of times, when a customer calls, you're not exactly sure what you're going to say. And not knowing what you're going to say can really trip you up. The customer is calling for a reason – they have a need. You want to guide them to a solution that involves using YOUR business, but coming up with the right words on the fly isn't easy for most people.

Developing scripts to use on the phone is one of the best things you can do.

By following a script, you can guide the customer through the process toward finding the right solution to their problem. You'll never have to worry about what to say next – because it's right there in the script. When you remember to show the value of your experience and talk about your price as an investment, saving them time, or preventing a problem, you won't have the need to discount your price.

Follow the Script...Part 2

Since the real gold in any business is your customer and prospect list, be sure to have a script to capture that information. Have you ever called a company and they said, "In case we get disconnected, may I have your name and phone number?" before they even began to answer your question? They've already followed a script to begin capturing details for their database.

Follow the Script...Part 3

Scripts can also be effective in person, although you obviously don't want to be reading what you say off of an actual script. But how many times have you walked away from a meeting and realized, "Oh, I wish I said ...?" A script can help you avoid that scenario. Start by thinking through how the conversation is likely to go, what questions and issues are likely to come up, and put those "Oh, I should have said this" comments down on paper. Familiarize yourself and your employees with those stock answers, and you'll be ready when the question or situation comes up.

The more you practice these phrases, the more smoothly and elegantly you'll be able to handle communicating with your customers. You'll be that much better at positioning your product or service as the best solution to your customer's problem or challenge. One of the questions to ask yourself is "what benefit is the customer really getting?"

Get Personal

You should set yourself apart and make an effort to be genuinely interested in your clients. When calling them, ask about personal things first. What do they care about most? Send them newspaper clippings of things that might be of interest - free tickets to an event are always a welcomed gesture. With the rise of social media, you could even hold a drawing and announce the winning client by posting a video of the winner's name being drawn to your Facebook page.

Get Personal – Part 2

A California Pizza Kitchen decided to have each of their employees wear pins that announced their individual hometown; this lead to interesting conversations between the wait staff and customers.

At Disney all the cast members wear badges with their country of origin.

Take a Ritzy Approach

If you've ever stayed at the Ritz Carlton, you undoubtedly have experienced first-class service. It's all about the "gold standard" that includes pocket-sized cards with their 20 corporate guiding principles. Every employee is empowered to "own" the guest's problem. Ladies and gentlemen serving ladies and gentlemen. It's all about the customers experience by "putting on the Ritz."

Show off with Cinch Cast
(Story from Jamahl Keyes)

I love Cinchcast.com. I'm a speaker and I love to talk so Cinchcast gives me that speaking platform every day, all day. I can send my customers a link to my how-to information in the form of an audio clip. People can even download it on their phones at Cinchcast.com.
If you've never heard of Cinchcast, let me explain:

(From the Cinchcast website)

> *"Cinchcast is a social network with an interesting twist — you can post status updates, add pictures and most importantly add audio! You are familiar with the micro-blogging poster child Twitter, right? Well Cinch Cast is like "audio micro-blogging". You get the same 140 characters or less to share your opinion and marketers can promote their product, service or organization. The beauty of this platform is you are able to utilize audio, and add pictures to share your message."*

And it can work for anyone. If you're a plumber, you can talk about the most frequently asked questions you get – the exact questions someone who needs a plumber probably has. If you're a lawyer, you can share your top 10 answers to basic legal questions. You're not just screaming "hire me, hire me, hire me" at your prospective clients; you're actually educating them and building trust!

Be a Video Star

You Tube is an amazing marketing tool that's also FREE! People love to talk to people...and this is as close to a conversation as you can possibly get without actually being with the person. You can structure your video however you want to. You can just talk to the camera, script something funny or informative, or even hire a professional to put together a mini movie or commercial with graphics and music. Attach it to your website and e-mail it to your current customers.

PART

6

Show Your Gratitude

Your existing customers are your most valuable customers because they already know what your business does and they've already hired you to do it. So a big part of your marketing time and effort should be dedicated to thanking those customers for using your business. A simple thank-you isn't just good manners – it also reminds your customers of the valuable services you provide! On the other hand, a more elaborate thank-you can rank as something a special client may never forget.

Write a *Handwritten* Note

In this age of email, there's nothing quite as special as a personal, handwritten note.

Handwritten notes are really a lost art. But they make the biggest impact! They tell the recipient that you cared enough to stop your busy day, sit down and actually pick up a pen (who does that these days?) and put your gratitude in writing.

Better yet, have your own cards made. It's simple, it's inexpensive, and it leaves a lasting impression. Don't be surprised if it's kept for years.

Play Santa

Every year, take time to thank your customers by personally delivering a Christmas/holiday plate and thank-you card. Depending on the person, you could make some cookies or get some fruit (some people are on diets!) and make a plate of treats; then hand-write a thank-you card and take it to them.

Your customers will know you put some effort into the gift and note, so it will be even more appreciated than just receiving a card in the mail.

Celebrate Alternative Holidays

Don't send Christmas cards. Instead, send Thanksgiving Day cards or Christmas cards in July. You'll get their attention for being the only one.

Or Better Yet...Create Your *Own* Holiday!

Maybe you've seen them in the paper or in a monthly newsletter – lists of obscure holidays that you can't believe are actually holidays. Yes, there's a Clean Out Your Refrigerator Day, a Hug Your Cat Day, and a World Turtle Day, but you can have your own holiday as well!

All you have to do is head over to the Chase's Calendar of Events online site (http://www.mhprofessional.com/templates/chases) and submit your entry. Chase provides a day-by-day directory of nationwide festivals, celebrity birthdays, historical anniversaries, culinary celebrations, entertainment awards, astronomical phenomena, presidential proclamations, and much more. So why not create an "official" holiday based around your business and then launch a special promotion around it? If you can't think of anything, you can always go to www.brownielocks.com and pick something.

Show Your Face

One small business owner found a pretty unique way to stand out from all those regular emails that crowd their customers' in boxes. When they want to say thank you, a video email puts their voice, their face, and everything all into one. I think it makes the thank-you that much more powerful because the recipient can see them, hears them, and actually experiences their emotion as if they were saying thank you in person.

Plus, it's just kind of cool!

Take Action Photos
(Story from Willis Yoder)

Being different helps my auction business stand out from the competition. We take pictures during the auction of all the action - the crowd, the buyers, and as many pictures of our customers as possible.

Then we print the photos and send a handwritten note to congratulate them for being a winning bidder, and thank them for choosing you to do business with you – it is appreciated.

I also put those pictures in a frame along with the auction brochure, our auction logo, and our contact information and put the customer's name on the bottom.

Our customers hang those pictures up with pride and tell all their friends(referrals) about their great find – so I'm not only providing great service to my existing customers, but I'm also exposing my business to new ones.

This "frame" idea can work in any business. Get creative.

You've Been Framed!

If you have a LOT of clients or customers, it can be expensive to reward them all. Use a system that gets you the most bang for your buck by singling out those customers who are the most valuable to you (i.e., they spend the most money or are your "A" customers). Our rewards system already tracks which of our customers spend the most money, so this particular year, we went through the list and took the top 100 customers and sent them a tin full of homemade peanut brittle along with a nice handwritten thank-you card. But we don't send them at Christmas. We pick an unusual, wacky, fun holiday and celebrate with them on that day.

It was unexpected. It was thoughtful. And – most importantly- no one else did it! That's what made it such a WOW moment for them. Some of the top 100 showed their appreciation by sending us cards and emails thanking us. And a lot of customers came back and thanked us in person (which we preferred)!

In fact, since we sent the gift during a slow business period, during the next few months, which are usually our slow time, picked up.

See? It pays to be generous and surprise your most profitable customers.

Buy the Book

Books are a great gesture because if you choose the right one, you can sell yourself while showing a deserving client your gratitude. I send my important clients books as thank-you gifts and always include a short note that says something like, "This book reminded me of you." Or "Thanks a Million", or "Thought you would appreciate this." But in reality, I choose books that reinforce the value of using my business.

Be a Smart Cookie

Saying thank you doesn't have to always be done with a handwritten note or peanut brittle. How about a "gratitude cookie"?At www.zenrabbitcookies.com you can choose from a whole assortment of gratitude items.

Other sources of creative thank-you items are www.Cheryls.com, www. Brownies.com, and **www.SendOutCards. com/71230**.

If you microwave a fortune cookie, you can even slip in your own fortune and reclose it.

Welcome your Customers

One great way many businesses have found to thank new clients for choosing their business is by putting together a welcome package. Any kind of business can do this for their new patients, new clients, and new customers – just keep in mind that the cost of the package to you should be based on the value of the customer.

For example, if you own an ice cream shop, you might give a new customer a free cone to come back a second time. You're saying thank you and getting them to come back, all at the same time. And the cost is in the realm of possibility based on the money you'll generate getting them in the habit of buying ice cream cones.

However, if you're a doctor or dentist, you might not be able to afford to give away free treatments. Some offer free consultations or low-cost treatments, and others put together a package of information, including CDs, DVDs, and pens,so that the patient gets something that they would not normally expect.

Of course, not all giveaways pay off, so make sure yours stands out and makes the customer remember you and gives them a reason to come back or refer you.

Reward Their Loyalty
(Story from John Cohoat)

I know this isn't anything revolutionary, but sometimes the simplest, no-brainer things are the things people neglect. And I'd venture to say most companies aren't using a loyalty rewards program, even though they know they should.

When I owned a local restaurant,I worked with a vendor who provided a computer program, a website, and swipe cards (and everything else we needed) to help us provide a very high-level rewards program.

As people came in, they were asked if they'd like to sign up for the rewards program. We explained some of the benefits that they would get, like free birthday dinners and free anniversary dinners. And eventually we had about 2,500 people in our rewards program, which was pretty darn good for our size of restaurant.

Using the system, we were able to market to these customers while thanking them and rewarding them for their loyalty. We would send them weekly emails and specials – and they would come back and spend more money! And they usually don't celebrate their birthday by themselves, so they'd bring friends and family.

Which is what I call a win-win?

Go the Extra Mile

Every area of the country has something unique and special about it. Visitors to that area would like to experience that uniqueness. There is a large Amish population in northern Indiana, which is of interest to a lot of people. Others would like to experience a meal in an Amish home. If you own a business that caters to tourists, why not develop concierge program/packages and add a new income source to your business? Own a bed and breakfast in an Amish community? Arrange for meals in an Amish home and take them there in a buggy, or visit some community theaters in the area, or arrange tours of local businesses like a winery or a name brand corporation.

PART

7 **Express Yourself**

In order to succeed in marketing, you need to remind the people who do business with you, and those who might do business with you, that you exist! Give them a reason to remember you. Sometimes, seeing something in print that comes from you will be all they need to remind them that it's time to get their teeth cleaned, or their car serviced, or have whatever you do done.

Plus, the more you put yourself and your personality out there for prospective customers to see, the more of them you'll attract. So here are a few ideas that should help you get started.

Change Your Name – Tag!

If you frequently attend seminars and business conferences, you're all-too-familiar with those bland stick-on name tags that fall off and reduce you to your hastily scribbled first name. Well, this is another opportunity to make more of an impact and stand out from the crowd.

Simply make your own name tag before you come to the event and bring it with you! It's easy to do – you can buy printable ones at Staples or Office Depot – and you can personalize it with your logo, your business nickname (for example, if you use a name like "The Newsletter Guy"), a picture of your actual product or service, whatever you want.

You name it and it's a marketing opportunity – even a simple name tag!

You can also buy a sheet for your computer printer that makes an iron on patch that you can print right from your computer. Or simply have a shirt embroidered with your business name. I used to think it would be tacky to wear a logo shirt to a church function, until I saw others wear their business shirt which gave me an excuse to start a conversation with them and ask about their business. So it really makes you more approachable in a crowd.

When Is a Card Not a Card?

The answer to this question is that a card is not a card when it's a mug, a clock, a mouse pad, a coin, or anything else.

And, to be even clearer, we're talking about your business card. If you're giving your customers an item at Christmas or whenever, make sure your business card imprint, with all your contact info, is included. And also try to make that item something that either sits on their desk or that they use daily. That means they will continually see your business name whenever they use it, creating nonstop subliminal marketing for you on a year-round basis, as well as building a referral culture!

Here's the front and back of a business card coin I designed and minted for Jim Connelly. Guaranteed people do not throw away his business card (coin).

Watch Your Backside

Before you get the wrong idea, I'm talking about the backside of your business card. Most people use only the front side for their contact information and leave the back blank – and that's a mistake. When we're talking about something that you're handing out on pretty much a daily basis, we're talking about something you utilize to the max by going to the flip side and adding your marketing motto, some branding imagery, or even a special first-time customer offer.

Blank space won't sell you, but an impactful message, motto, or offer will!

Share the News

People love getting mail. Real mail. Brought to them and hand delivered to their mailbox by a real live human. I've never met anyone who gets tired of checking the mail. Use that to your advantage. Publish a self-produced newsletter with fun things, pictures, and just a little about your company. Don't make it boring, and customers will look forward to getting it every month.

Now, with today's technology it's too easy to send an email or a message on Facebook, or do something electronically. Almost nobody spends the time and the money to put something physical in people's mailboxes. Which means that when you do, you stand out!

For example, if I were a dentist, I wouldn't talk about dentistry in my newsletter. Not at all. I mean, how many times do you need to know that you need to floss your teeth and need to get them cleaned twice a year? So I wouldn't talk about that.

Instead, I'd make my pet a celebrity and talk to people from the pet's point of view. I'd add puzzles and games. I'd add whatever I had to, to make it fun and educational...so people would want to read it.

If you are a roofing contractor, you are eliminating a customer for 25 or 30 years when you do work for them. But if you send them a periodic newsletter that shows them how to protect that roof to make it last longer (ie. Fall schedule to caulk roof vents and skylights, clean the gutters, and make sure down spouts divert water away from foundation to keep moisture from migrating into attic), they will think of you in two years when their neighbors need a new roof. And this newsletter should let them know if you are adding a new service like gutter installations, or skylight installations.

I have an easy to use newsletter template service that my customers LOVE. Each month I design a 4 page newsletter template using Microsoft Publisher and make it available to my clients to customize and edit and turn into their own newsletter for mailing to their clients, customers, and patients. Check it out at **www. megabucksmarketing.com/newsletter-templates.**

Cash In on Your Brain

When you're in business (or doing anything) for a certain period of time, you become an expert at what you do. You know it inside and out, better than the majority of people in the whole, entire world.

Well, if you put your information – all those things you know about what you do - down on paper, suddenly you have an information product ready to be packaged. And that's a product you can sell.

That's how this book came about. It's a collection, a master mind collaboration of my best proven marketing strategies as well as some of the best ideas my entrepreneur friends have used successfully, and were willing to share.

Write a Book

If you're anything like me or my colleagues who worked on this book with me, you know enough about the business you're in to write a book.

Well, I'm living proof that you actually can write that book – and I'm writing this particular tip because I also happen to believe you should.

If you were researching a professional – say, a dentist – on the Internet and one of the contenders had actually written a book about the very procedure you were interested in, wouldn't that boost your interest and confidence in that dentist? Write a book and suddenly you are an expert, standing head and shoulders above all your non-book-writing competitors.

I know what you're probably thinking right now, "I don't know how to write a book." Not a problem. One of the services I offer is to write books for clients. It doesn't have to be the next best American novel. Just that you write one is important.

Once your book is written, you can have it published and give it away to clients, allow people to download it as an e-book off your website, or even sell it on a website like Amazon.com. And if you give it to a prospective client, it's like handing them the ultimate resume, showcasing everything you know and do!

These are two books I have been commissioned to write for a New York Attorney. Notice the cartoons!

If you need ideas for a book, writing an e-book on how to do something is a great place to start. I know a landscaper who wrote an e-book on landscaping hospital grounds, and hospitals now call him in for interviews and just say, "Okay. When can you start?" They already know what he can do, and they are sold. Wow!

Be a Cover Girl (or Guy)

Maybe you're not quite ready for the cover of Forbes or Fortune. But you can still have your 15 minutes on the cover of a magazine by having a tear sheet done.

In case you don't know what a tear sheet is – and chances are, you don't! – I should probably explain. A tear sheet is a piece of marketing material that looks and reads like a real magazine article, and it's written all about you and your business! The style is exactly the same as a magazine article, and it's laid out like a real magazine piece, including an official-looking magazine cover with your photo and headlines about you, your business, and related fields. It talks about the highlights in your life, and your personal interests, so your customer can relate to you and like you. Did I mention that people buy from people they like?

It's not written in a bragging way. Instead, it's written just like a reporter did an article on you, but it says exactly what you want to get across to your readers with no interpretation from the reporter. And it's laid out with lots of photos, pull-out lines and quotes, and even a chart, so it's fun and interesting to read.

The result? You're now positioned as an expert.

So if you're an Avon lady, what makes you different from any other Avon salesperson? If you hand a prospect a tear sheet, suddenly they have a glossy, well-written magazine piece that will explain exactly who you are and why you do what you do. You can also have newspaper tear sheets, which look just like you were featured in a local or national newspaper.

It's easy to have them done.
Go to **www.MegabucksMarketing.com/Done-4-You-Magazine**

Post Articles

One great way to position yourself as an expert in the public eye is to write articles about topics in your field. You don't even have to worry about sending them around to magazines or websites – there are plenty of article sites that will help you through the process of posting your writing and positioning yourself as an authority.

How does it work? Well, let's say you're a lawyer and you're hoping to grow your law firm by attracting some new clients. If you have how-to articles explaining the areas of law you practice (with your contact info on the bottom) sprinkled all over the Internet and other lawyers at other firms don't, who do you think stands out as the expert?

Articles also work well for recent college graduates. Technology is always changing, so a lot of college students are learning the latest ways of doing things, as opposed to how it was done 10 or 15 years ago when most of the people hiring were educated. So, by writing articles on some of the cutting-edge stuff you just learned, you show companies that you can add value to their organization. By doing this, you position yourself as an asset...and that's huge!

Double Down

Before I take the time to put any marketing message in writing, I do what I call a "check scan." That's just my term for taking a moment to consider the type of reader who is going to be reading that sales message – whether it's going out in the form of an ad, a direct mail piece, a blog on my website, whatever.

I know some readers will simply glance at my message, and if they don't see something interesting in that first nanosecond, they're gone. Other people are much more detail-oriented and will read every word from beginning to end. So I try to make sure whatever I send out is talking to both of them. For the scanners,I use headings with bold letters, highlights, copy doodles, and handwritten notes,and I circle certain items I really want them to notice. For the detail checkers, I use all of the above to draw them in and then give them all I've got so they stay and read as much as possible!

Meet the Press

The news media is like somebody who can't get full no matter how much they eat. Every day, they start from scratch, needing fresh content on the latest and greatest to fill space on tight schedules and, these days, on even tighter budgets.

That's where you can find an opening to promote yourself and what you do. It's one of those win-win situations because you get a dose of prestige publicity from appearing in a genuine news publication, and they get reputable, useful content that's completely done for them.

For example, say you're a chef. You might want to write an article every week about eating healthy since it's a hot topic that people are incredibly interested in these days. Now, in those articles, you wouldn't be able to directly sell your services or your restaurant, if you had one; that's considered an advertisement and publications charge businesses for those. However, you can subtly showcase your recipes and your business, just in the course of your educational articles. For example, you might talk about your citrus salad recipe and add, "By the way, this is one of our most popular lunch dishes at my restaurant, The Main Street Bistro."

Whatever your niche may be, if you can provide consumer-friendly advice or information about it, you'll have a good shot at getting in your local publication or online information site. Not only is this awesome free advertising, but you'll find your image is automatically elevated in the eyes of the public when you're presented in a way that looks like you were the best expert they sought out to ask about this subject. It's as if the media conferred expert status on you themselves!

Get on TV!

Getting yourself on TV is yet another way to stand out head-and-shoulders above the competition. Local access and cable shows, and even your local network affiliate (CBS, NBC, ABC, or FOX), could be looking for someone just like you, especially if you have a niche that's appealing to a lot of TV viewers and everyday consumers. Don't want to go the traditional route? Produce your own

My friend, David Cathers, is a real estate agent in Washington who started his own online TV show.

DavidCathers.tv
Easy Real Estate Videos

online tv show like my friend, David Cathers.

Steve Latour of Washington, D.C., is a good example of how an everyday entrepreneur can make it big on the boob tube. Residents there know him more commonly as "The Lei Man." Latour was looking for a unique and attention-getting approach to market his handmade Hawaiian leis and managed to talk the local public access channel into giving him his own TV show, *Lei Man's World.*

Of course, the next problem was that

he couldn't just spend the entire TV time slot advertising his leis – he needed some actual content! So, while he and his friends wore his handmade leis around their necks (advertisement enough!), they reviewed food, wine, and new movies. His inspiration? An old movie! "I was looking for a cheap way to advertise," said Latour. "And then I saw *Wayne's World.*" But the newly crowned "Lei Man" didn't forget to ask for the order. Callers who phone in to his show to comment on the topics are also asked if they want to order a lei as well!

Make Friends with Facebook

And speaking of media, as you are already well aware, it's not all about print, radio, and TV anymore. Social media's popularity continues to skyrocket, and the biggest player in that arena is Facebook. You'll be surprised at how much you're able to engage both your current customers as well as future prospects when you initiate interactions on social media platforms.

For example, I recently heard that the fastest growing segment in Facebook is women between the ages of 35 and 60. Now, if that's your business demographic and you're not marketing yourself on Facebook, imagine what an opportunity you're missing out on. But, again, that's just the fastest-growing demographic – the millions of Facebook users are comprised of all ages and incomes and are an incredibly valuable audience to promote yourself to.

That's why you should consider creating a fan page for your business on Facebook. If

click like →

RESOURCES →

NINA HERSHBERGER

Outrageous Marketer,
Author, Coach,
and Action Taker

New book due out November 1st!

you're not all that familiar with Facebook, you should know there are two types of pages: personal ones, where you interact with friends and share things happening in your life, and fan pages, which are more for your company or business.

Now, when I say fan pages are for your business, I don't mean you should leave your personality completely out of it. You still want people to relate to who you are, but you want to mix that up with business offers, contests, useful content and videos, or just other fun and interesting projects you're working on. You can also solicit video testimonials from customers or positive postings from other entrepreneurs or companies you work with.

To me, a Facebook fan page positions you better than almost anything else out there. Whether you're a business owner providing a solution to the public or a student getting ready to look for a job, it's an easy and impactful way to promote yourself – and best of all, it's free!

Tweet with Twitter

While it can be a little more difficult to get your marketing points across with 140 characters or less (the current limit of the size of a tweet – which is what a message you send across Twitter is called), Twitter is still a very valuable social media tool to hook up with. Again, you're extremely limited in terms of content, recommendations and so forth, but you can post links to your content and products, as well as network with people that know other influential people (which is the key premise behind the bestselling book "Tipping Point").

Twitter can also be important in terms of visibility – the more active you appear, the more successful and impressive you seem. And keep in mind there are free applications such as Tweetdeck and Hootsuite that allow you to tweet and simultaneously use the same tweet to update your Facebook status as well.

So...get out there and start using social sites to be seen.

LinkedIn is another professional social media site with an ever-increasing number of users. Just remember, social media is a side dish, but never the main entrée. You need to use all available tools to market yourself successfully – and social media is just another one of those tools (but an important one!). Don't ever rely on just one marketing method, because things change and you could find yourself playing catch up.

PART

9

Making the Most of Mail

If you haven't noticed, your mailbox has been growing more and more empty with each delivery over the past few years. As postage rises and more and more free and convenient online communications are developed, most businesses and individuals find the postal service to be slow, expensive, and unnecessary.

But that decline actually offers an important opportunity. That's because people still love to get mail – and anything *you* send is going to stand out more than ever. Whereas junk mail used to be an automatic candidate for the trash, in today's world, a direct mail campaign is now an excellent way to stand out from the herd and target your desired audience.

There's also a certain value now associated with direct mail that wasn't there before. The recipient knows you've spent real money, real postage, and real effort to send it, unlike an email.

Put Lumps in the Mailbox!

To me, the best thing about direct mail is that it's really fun because you can send real 3-D stuff! You can add what I call "grabbers" pennies, pens, erasers, etc. – to make your mailing enticingly lumpy or dimensional. You can also play with envelopes that really stand out, such as using different colors or shapes that will surprise the recipient.

For instance, one famous direct mail piece is one in which the envelope looks just like a wallet. Why is it so effective? Well, when people see something that looks like a wallet, the first thing they want to do, is open it!!!

The best thing about the wallet piece is that it only requires one first class stamp, unlike most creative mail pieces. It's the perfect combination that puts together everything I want to see in a direct mail piece – it's attention-getting, it prompts the recipient to see what's inside, and it's incredibly cost-effective. You can add money looking coupons with your face on the bill and even a sales letter. For more information on this unique direct mail piece, go to **www.WalletMailer.com**

Create a Résumé with Resonance

Cover letters and resumés tend to follow the same old boring black and white typed formats, which means yours can frequently get lost in the shuffle.

Well, there are ways to up the creative quotient even on these by-the-book items. For example, here's an idea I gave to one of my clients that ended up working like gangbusters for him; it's an idea that really anyone can use.

My client was applying for a job with a gentleman we'll call "John Smith." He began by creating a cover letter with a headline that read, "Just what the doctor ordered for John Smith!"

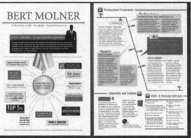

He then took that cover letter, folded it along with his résumé, and put it inside a prescription medicine container. He then mailed that bottle to John Smith.

Why have a boring resume? Bert Molner's is anything but boring.

Do you think that got John Smith's attention? Do you think he would open a medicine container he received in the mail that had no other explanation attached to it? Of course he did – and it helped my client stand out from all the other job applicants, by showcasing his personality and creative approach to the situation.

Naturally, this kind of idea can be used to get anyone's attention for any reason. If you're trying to reach a busy individual who's too pressed for time to even respond, a gimmick like this can do the trick.

And that's what it's really all about – showing some creativity and individuality, as well as breaking the boring old molds of the past. Marketing that stands out is designed to stand out, so always think about how you can take these kinds of everyday situations to a whole new level. Most self-help memory boosting programs talk about adding outrageous action to what you are trying to remember. So do this for your customers to help them remember you. You'll find some more examples in the next few tips.

Research Brings Rewards
(Story from Bert Molner)

Another way to reach someone influential is to do a little legwork on their likes and dislikes.

In the example I'm about to share, it was actually more footwork than legwork. One client wanted to reach the head of a firm who was famous for being hard to get a hold of. So he embarked on a plan to find out more about the business owner and to use that information to his benefit.

He discovered that the business owner wore a certain unique make of shoes. So he went out and bought the exact same kind of shoes, and put *only* one of those shoes inside a box, along with a letter. What did the letter say? Well, obviously, it opened with, "I'm just trying to get my foot in the door." It then went on to talk about what my client could do for the head of the company and finished with, "I hope we can set up a meeting shortly. Because when I get the chance to see you in person, I'll gladly hand over the companion to the shoe in this box."

As you can imagine, my client got a call from the owner within a few days of mailing the shoe and the letter. It's always worth researching whomever you're pursuing for a deal or a job. The more you know, the more you can use to sell yourself to them creatively in a way that will stand out with them, because they are already interested in it.

Put Out an APB

If you sense that you're losing touch with someone whom you don't want to lose touch with, then the best thing to do is to find a fun way to regain their attention.

Here's a method that can set you apart. Take a picture of yourself looking off into the distance with a quizzical look on your face, as if you're trying to find something and can't seem to locate it. Your expression should be silently saying, "Where is...?" If you have kids, have them join in the photo if they can summon up the same kind of expression on their faces.

Take that photo and either create a postcard out of it or place the photo at the top of a letter. Mail the letter or postcard to the person you want to get back in touch with you with some clever copy, such as, "I've been looking for you for awhile now."

This idea is a clever and amusing way to let someone special know that you miss them and want to talk to them. It could be to get a lost customer back into your store or to get someone important and influential back into your circle. Whatever the situation, it can defuse tension and prompt a welcome phone call or visit from the person in question. After all, the second easiest customer to gain is a lost customer.

Searching for Contacts

Another fun way to remind a person that they haven't been in touch with you lately is to use a "lumpy" direct mail piece that includes a magnifying glass (make sure the "glass" is actually plastic, though!) inside the envelope. Include a letter with the magnifying glass that talks about how you've been looking for them every way you know how.

Because the envelope obviously holds a physical object, the person receiving it will invariably open it. And, again, they will probably be amused by this gambit to regain their attention and make them think, "Whoa, I should really get back with this person, since they went to all this trouble for me!" That's the rule of reciprocity. When you do something nice for them, they psychologically feel obligated to do something nice for you.

Have a Ball

Afraid a relationship or business association is over because of a lack of response from someone? Here's a way to see if it can bounce back from the brink.

By mailing a rubber ball inside a package with a note that begins with the sentence, "Hope I didn't drop the ball," you're both acknowledging you may have done something wrong in a humorous way and also inviting the person to give you another try. The letter would go on to quickly say, "Just touching base with you. Just a quick reminder..."then it should mention something specific about the situation.

This kind of mailing can make the person receiving the ball (by the way, the ball makes for another great attention-getting lumpy mailing!) think twice about their relationship with you. For example, they may not remember why they stopped being in touch with you and think, "Wait a minute, did I forget to call him? Was I the one who dropped the ball?"

Make it stand out

When I want to make sure my proposal or pitch stands out from the rest of the crowd, I like to grab the recipient's attention with a relevant piece of lumpy mail. One trick I've used is wrapping up a pair of tube socks and using a headline like "This will knock your socks off!" on the cover letter. After all, how many proposals come complete with a pair of socks? Or what about send an x-ray in the mail? Or a popcorn bag?

Turn Trash into Treasure
(Story from Dan Brekke)

In every business there are scraps and throwaways. It stands to reason that if you own a metal etching company, like Indiana Metal Etching in Elkhart, IN, you'd have scrap metal. Yes, it gets recycled, but one day it struck us to create our 3" x 5" business cards out of metal. Add a couple of etched samples on the card and we had something really unique and interesting.

Can you say "home run"?

We've now done metal business cards for all kinds of big-shots, from company presidents to mayors of Chinese provinces. We've also done a heck of a lot of them for individuals who want to stand out from the crowd and be noticed.

One client who was in the financial business had us create a business card for him that looked like a thin gold bar.

The thing that makes these cards so powerful is that, unlike regular crappy paper business cards, people don't throw these away. They keep them, they always know where they are (unlike a paper business card), and they show them to friends. And sometimes they even order them! What business are you in? What should you be using for a business card?

PART

10

Going Where the Money Is

Most businesses think marketing is all about chasing new customers. However, we've learned through experience that the most important customers to market to are the ones you already have.

That's because of the common business aphorism, Pareto's Principle, which states that 80% of your income comes from 20% of your clients. Business-management consultant Joseph M. Juran coined the phrase and named it after Italian economist Vilfredo Pareto, who observed in 1906 that 80% of the land in Italy was owned by 20% of the population.

That 80/20 rule means that you should spend some extra time and effort – maybe even the bulk of your time and effort – marketing to that top tier of your client list. After all, these are the people who are more likely to buy, *more* likely to buy more, and more likely to recommend you to their friends and relatives.

Here are a few things we've tried to reach our best (most profitable) – and potentially best – customers.

Make Your "A", B", and "C" List

If you're planning to market to your top customers, the first thing you need to do is identify them. A good customer list divides customers into categories. There are the A customers whom you couldn't live without (they will be significant to your business profits in the next 12-24 months), the B customers who give you their business fairly regularly, and the C customers who use your services once in awhile, and then there are customers you wish you could get rid of completely.

With a good list, you can start applying the 80/20 principle without a hassle. You'll know exactly who those top customers are so you can get down to the important business of romancing them and keeping them happy!

Focus most of your efforts in romancing the A clients and upgrading the B customers to A status. Your assistant can spend their time on the B customers, and the C customers would get the automatic mailers, or annual contact (more self-service and less of your valuable personal time).

Go Whale Hunting

Five years from now, who would be some of the dream clients you would like to have in your business? If you want a better business 5 years from now, you need to purposely make time to attract those clients (instead of reacting to activities of the day). Which is why Thursday you might designate as "Whale Hunting Day". Every Thursday block out an appointment time and engage in some one-on-one marketing with these potential big clients.

When you come into the office on Monday, if you haven't set an appointment for your Whale Hunting Thursday, make that the highest priority for the beginning of your week.

Script "Hi Bob, this is _____. I plan to be in your area Thursday and would like to take you to lunch to catch up. How does _____ restaurant sound?"

Pick one of three potentials:
1) a top prospect you would like to do business with
2) a current top 5% client, who you invite to bring a friend
3) a key referral source who has strong relationships with the best kind of clients you want to attract. (Did you know that referred clients are eight times more likely to do business with you? If the prospect is referred by a trusted advisor, I believe that closing rate is much, much higher.)

On Thursday, treat the lunch itself as a social occasion – don't bring proposals or samples. It's strictly a time to relax, talk about family, how they got started in the business, and enjoy a break from the office.

And it works. Doing this one thing each week will have one of the best positive impacts on your business to leap over your competition.

Move Your Meeting
(Story from Bert Molner)

Sometimes the best thing you can do is meet where the client is going to be the most relaxed and open. Even if that means meeting in the great outdoors!

There was a time I was trying to land our biggest account to date – and that meant I had to make sure I could close the deal with the prospect in question. I had a meeting set up at his office, but then the wheels in my head started turning, as they often do.

I found out this guy liked duck hunting and actually had a big duck blind on some property he had bought. The boss I was working for at the time enjoyed duck hunting too, so instead of a stuffy business meeting in a bland conference room, we moved the confab over to the duck blind in the morning.

That made for a different kind of business meeting – the kind where hunting dogs are a part of the equation. But a special kind of bonding happened as we ended up talking about his wife and kids, how his parents had started the business, and where the company was now. That naturally transitioned (and the key word here is *naturally*) into talking about what set his company apart from the competition and how we could leverage that.

We ended up landing that account and getting a lot more business from the client than we'd ever imagined, and we didn't have to discount our services at all.

Now, had this been a traditional business meeting, the typical power struggle negotiation where everyone has their defenses up. It would have been his suits across the table from our suits in a cold, deliberate negotiation that probably would have ended up with us discounting to a lower price – if we had gotten the account at all. Instead, the personal relationship came first and drove the business relationship. It developed as a very strong personal relationship (to this day) with each of us getting to know and care about the other.

Approach is everything. Keep that in mind when courting any big-money client.

Pick Up the Check – When You're Not Even There!

This tip also may require a little research and involves a small pay-off from you that could result in a much bigger one down the line.

Let's say there's a person you're trying to court for a business deal or job. And, somehow, you know which restaurant that person frequents. Now, if you can find out *when* that person is eating at that restaurant (you can actually just call and see if there's a reservation in their name), you've got a chance to make your mark.

Simply arrange with the restaurant to pay for the person's meal, but also arrange not to let them know until it's time to get the check. Then, instead of the check, arrange to have a package delivered with your resume or proposal and a cover letter that says, "Time is money, so, hopefully, if I pay for your dinner, I can earn a few minutes of your time."

What you've done is obligated this person to take you seriously and review your paperwork with all due consideration. You've separated yourself from the herd in a very memorable and impactful way.

It worked for a contractor who was after a contract from the head of a company. The contractor ended up getting not only the contract, but also some other extra business. The man he bought dinner for never forgot that maneuver and always brought it up whenever they got together. It's a kind of unforgettable "personal branding" that always makes you top-of-mind with the people you want to influence.

Play it Safe!
(Story from Bert Molner)

Maybe you can't tell a book by its cover, but if you make that cover just as awesome as possible, the book may not even matter!

If you're a salesperson who works for a corporation, some of the marketing materials you're provided can be incredibly generic and boring. That's something you usually can't control, but you still have to do your job and make new sales. The question then becomes how do you work around what you're required to give to a prospect and still "wow" them?

This is a case where you have to literally think outside the box. Actually, to be more accurate, you have to think *about* the box. Maybe you can't control the content, but you *can* control the delivery mechanism.

One wealthy gentleman whose business I wanted inspired me to put the marketing materials inside an actual combination safe, a very heavy-duty fireproof one. It was so heavy that shipping it would have been very expensive and risky, so I dropped it off myself at his office.

Well, number one, those generic marketing materials didn't get brushed off – mainly because the guy couldn't even get to them! There was only a note attached to the outside of the safe which read, "Call me for the combination to the valuable contents."

Now, you're thinking, "Even if he opens the safe, there's still all that boring stuff in there." That's why we had another surprise up our sleeves. When his office called for the combination, we gave it to them, and when they opened the safe, they didn't just find those dreaded by-the-numbers brochures. They also found a dinner invitation to a beautiful exclusive country club, with another note that read, "I'd like an opportunity to chat with you and your wife over an amazing dinner to discuss how I can be of benefit to you." There was also a personal biography of my own accomplishments attached to that note, along with an elegant special menu the executive chef had prepared.

This is a technique that has worked three times for me, and all three times it worked with people who were notoriously difficult to get a meeting with, and who probably get generic sales literature from my competitors several times a week. As always, the packaging makes a difference and makes you stand out.

Oh, and did I mention that his "gate keeper" assistant told me not to bother sending anything when I called to confirm the address, because there was no way anyone was getting on his busy schedule.

Double Your Pleasure

Personal relationships, as I always say, are critical to successful business. And when you're courting your top clients, the more you can get involved in their circle, the better.

That's why when you want to entertain an important person by taking them to a play, a concert, a pro game, or any other special event;you don't just buy two tickets for that person and their spouse. Instead, give them four tickets so they can invite another couple they know.

First of all, you'll impress the person with your thoughtfulness and generosity. Second of all, you will now be able to meet the people they are closest to – people who generally are either relatives or in the same business circle. Whichever category they fit into, they will have influence on the person you want to impress.

The bigger ticket an event it is, the better it works. To wow your top clients, create "exclusive" magic moments for them to tell others about and allow them to share those moments with their friends and/or family. You'll find yourself suddenly becoming a part of their special circle. You'll get better attendance if you can arrange for something they normally could not do on their own, like a wine cellar barrel tasting with the vintner. Also, include a note that says "please return these tickets if you are not able to put them to use". Trust me, people will realize how valuable this rare experience is and not want to miss out. Always have your assistant call to confirm their attendance a day or two ahead of time. Always offer a very nice door prize so you can collect the information on the referred guests so you have a means of communicating and educating them for future business.

Fulfilling Needs

There's an old joke about two salesmen who were trying to sell paint to a town. The first salesman encounters the mayor, but the mayor is on his way out the door. He brusquely says, "I don't need any paint; we've had a bad car accident and I have to go see what happened."

The second salesman follows the mayor and discovers that the street where the accident occurred had experienced a lot of car collisions because it was a small town and they had never added stripes down the center of the roads. Motorists were continually crossing over into the oncoming traffic, because they couldn't tell where their half of the road was.

When that second paint salesman finally had his shot at the mayor, he successfully sold his paint. Why? Because he told the mayor he was selling stripes to prevent more accidents, not paint. And the mayor knew that was the one thing he did need.

Consider this silly little story because the moral of it isn't so silly. What's actually important to your current customers and future prospects? What do they really need, and how can you relate what you sell to their specific situation?

And, as always, this goes to the personal side, too. Whomever you need to impress, find out about their personal passions and hobbies. If they are dedicated to helping a particular charity, find a way to help that charity, too.

When you make yourself useful, people like having you around. And they want to work with you.

Go Ahead – Be a Drip!

"Folgers in Your Cup" is my name for drip marketing.

If you don't know what drip marketing is all about, it's regularly reminding people that you're around and giving them a reason to remember you at the same time. It's basically keeping up a relationship and letting clients know that you're thinking about them, little by little, and with steady frequency.

So look for reasons to communicate. For instance, if you see an article about something that a client, prospect or small group with similar interests will enjoy, email (but do not let them see that you sent it to a bunch of people) or "send them a copy with a short note. The personal touch is key and is something everybody talks about but few actually bother to do! And of course, birthdays, holidays, or personal family events such as graduations and marriages are excellent times to send an email or, better yet, a card through the mail.

You probably noticed from the above examples that these "drips" should not be sales pitches. It's something informative or of interest to *them*, so they know you care more about who they are than how much business they can give you.

That means you should know as much as you can about them on a personal level. That gives you more of the kind of knowledge that will trigger these "drip" occasions in your brain.

PART

11

Special Events

Creating your own special events and including your top clients is another way of bonding them personally to you. First of all, they're *your* special events, you're your customers won't be able to experience them without having you in the picture. Second of all, these special events showcase your creativity as well as your organizational ability to pull these things off.

Yes, special events can be a lot of work and expense for what might not look like any immediate short-term gain, but they're an integral part of your personal branding and making yourself memorable, as well as an important way to protect your herd of valuable customers that your competition wants to steal away. These are the people you want to impress and keep close to you.

Honor Your Herd

A special event can be, at its most basic level, simply hosting a barbeque, a cook-out, a fish fry, or some other everyday kind-of-gathering where you can feed your clients relatively cheaply in a relaxed and social environment. As you make the guest list and hold the event, you become the center of this particular universe and establish yourself as a connected networker who can put important people together.

A fun way to make it more than just another barbeque is to also make it a charity auction of some type (especially if an important client is affiliated with the charity). You can do good for others as well as for yourself!

Throw a Pareto

Instead of throwing a parade, throw a Pareto!

If you don't remember the name Pareto, he's the guy earlier in this book that Pareto's Principle was named after. Pareto's Principle is that 80% of your income most likely comes from 20% of your customers.

So why on earth would you focus only that 20% of your time on that high-end source of revenue? In business, and in life, some people are just more equal than others, and more enjoyable!

With that top 20% of your clients in mind, do a little research and try to determine what they have in common, including hobbies, charities, organizations, and places where they might mutually gather.

So, instead of throwing a barbeque for everyone (which is still a good idea once in awhile), throw a parade for your top 20% and tailor that parade to their common interests. It probably won't be an actual parade, but a specially-tailored event of some sort – so don't bother booking a marching band! If many of your top customers seem to enjoy classic cars, create an event. If many of them seem to enjoy fishing, create a big-fish outing.

Join Forces
(Story from Bert Molner)

91.

Sometimes it makes sense for you and another business to put together a win-win event that benefits both of you. I call these collaborations "Joint Ad-Ventures," but they're more commonly known as just plain joint ventures JVs. Generally, these occur when a local business helps me put on an event, knowing that they'll gain exposure to my more-moneyed clients.

For example, I had a client who, at the time, was about to open a winery in our area. I asked him if he would create a sneak-peek wine-tasting event for some of my top clientele before he held his actual grand opening. I presented this to my top 20% as an exclusive invitation-only private event, making it seem special. And of course, we sent four tickets to invite their favorite companions. That made me look great; meanwhile, my friend with the winery was able to personally sell my clients on his wine, giving them a wine-tasting straight out of the wine barrels in the cellar of the winery.

We also have in our area a very high-end movie entertainment store and audio/video store; one of their showrooms is a quarter-million-dollar home theater system that only seats eight people, making it the world's greatest private movie theatre. Once a month, we invite only two of our top client couples to a private exclusive screening of a new movie release. What does the owner of the hi-tech store get out of it? Well, he gets to show these well-off guests the latest and greatest technology that they just might buy on the spot, and my guests think they're getting their own private look at this cutting-edge stuff.

There are many other ways you can put together these kinds of JVs, where you get to impress your clients and your partner-business gets some up-close-and-personal selling time with them. The trick is that the business you team up with should be able to offer something cool and upscale to your clients; that way, your clients don't mind their sales pitch because it's about something they want to know more about it. You don't want it coming off as a sales pitch, but rather a demonstration of the latest and greatest that you've asked that business to show your friends.

The mistake you *shouldn't* make is making your own sales pitch during one of these special JVs. This is all about making a special impression on your clients and building up the personal relationship by getting to know them better, as well as meet their close friends. The more "exclusives" you offer them, the more they will want you in their orbit and the longer you'll be doing business with them.

Did I mention that the other businesses did not charge me anything for these events, and they introduced me to their loyal clients as well? In fact, the high end theatre store said he and his wife thought I should start bringing clients twice a month. "Why would you want to shut down your store on a Tuesday night and babysit just a few clients of mine, twice as often?" I asked. "Well", he said, "we just bought a $3,000 ad on the back cover of a custom housing publication, and that brought us in three new clients that ordered equipment. They were all a pain in the butt and tried to beat us up on price. On the other hand, several of your clients came back in and ended up ordering equipment as well. They also brought their friends in and said "you gotta see this place. Let me introduce you to the owner." They were looking for solutions to make their lifestyle more convenient and automated. None of them tried to beat us up on price, because they were introduced to us by you. And that only cost us a six pack of Coca-Cola."

Rent-A-Celebrity

Okay, so you're not exactly Brad Pitt or Angelina Jolie...yet. But, even if you're not an international celebrity yourself (again "yet!"), you can still use stardom to your advantage – just hire one!

Stars do bring customers in, and you might be surprised to learn just how inexpensive they can be. For example, most of you are probably familiar with the long-running reality TV series *Project Runway*. For those of you who aren't, the show begins with 16 fashion designer "contestants," and each week, one of them is eliminated until they finally crown a winner.

Project Runway Fan Favorite, Peach Carr, was a celebrity judge at an event I planned & executed for a client

On *Project Runway Season 8*, one of the fashion designers, Peach Carr, was an audience favorite, even though she didn't win the competition. She still had a big fan base, however, that could be used, and she lived relatively close to my cosmetic surgeon client who wanted to stage a celebrity event.

I partnered with Goodwill Industries to put on a repurpose runway show where local designers would repurpose donated Goodwill clothing, dress models in them, and send them down the runway.

Who became his celebrity judge? You guessed it – Peach Carr, at a very affordable price. She made a big splash and gave this surgeon an amazing amount of free publicity, which helped bring in new clients.

And don't worry about having to go through agents who will try to jack up the booking price for one of these semi-celebrities. Believe it or not, sometimes you can go right on Facebook and "friend" the celebrity, after which you can send them a private message with an offer and see if they respond. That's exactly how I made contact with Peach.

Nationwide Is
on Your Side
(Story from Dan Brekke)

With the rise of online communication, more businesses than ever have clients all across the country, rather than focused in the area around where the company is physically located.

The challenge, then, is how do you hold a relatively inexpensive event that includes all your various customers who are spread all across this great land of ours?

Well, a good way to begin is to hook up with something else that's nationwide, such as a restaurant chain. With that as your foundation, you can launch a national customer appreciation event.

Here's how I've done it in the past.

First, we mailed all of our customers a letter in a brown paper lunch bag telling them about the forthcoming event. That brown paper lunch bag, of course, got their attention and motivated them to read the letter.

Next, we chose a national pizza chain that would be able to deliver food to all of our customers – enough for them as well as their employees. We then verified the amount of food we needed for each location, including pizzas, salads, and beverages, and made sure the owner of the business let all the employees know that lunch for the day in question was going to be taken care of by us.

Finally, we sent a prep package that contained a letter to be read the day of the lunch delivery. That letter was designed to be a simple, fun message from us, thanking our customers for their loyalty and then offering them an irresistible offer that would give us more work from them.

This process basically brings a tremendous amount of value to clients that obligates them to listen to our newest pitch. Our customers didn't have to buy from us to get the pizza, but they felt like they should!

By the way, follow-up is always important, so in that prep package, I suggest you provide a small disposable digital camera for them to take pictures of their group enjoying the food, along with a postage-paid mailer that they could use to send the camera back to you. After the event, you can use those photos to put together a brochure or flier that thanks them for participating in your event.

Throw a Theme Night
(Story by John Cohoat)

Our ice cream company was a '50s-style drive-in restaurant. So, during the summer, we'd have themed nights - for example, Tuesday night would be cruise-in night, where we'd invite people to bring their classic cars to the restaurant and park them in a designated area where other customers could take a look at them.

To add to the fun, we'd also have specials for that night, maybe hotdogs for $1 or malts for $2. And a lot of the time, we'd hire a DJ or have a band.

Depending on what your business is, a theme night might be just the ticket to boost your customer base and get some extra publicity. Keep in mind that the best thing you can do is pick a theme that will hook into a thriving and affluent niche. The classic car owners fit that kind of niche because they want to show off their vehicles and they also are extremely loyal to businesses that allow them the spotlight as we did.

So...what niche can you attract with a theme night?

Show Your Spirit
(Story by John Cohoat)

We owned an inn that had a lot of land around it, 18 acres all together. And it just so happened that my son really loves fireworks, so you can imagine how much excitement the 4th of July means to him.

Luckily, fireworks are legal where the inn was, so we financed our son's own personal fireworks show for our guests. He would buy them at a local store, and we'd announce a special show the night of the 4th. The show itself would last about 45 minutes, with a grand finale that left everyone thrilled and happy. We also built a campfire and roasted marshmallows and made s'mores for our guests.

The annual event was a fun, patriotic time for us, as well as a "wow" moment and unforgettable experience for guests. And the fact that our son did it all on his own made it all the more memorable. It made the guests feel part of our family and also made them likely to return! What a great story for the newsletter!

Showcase Your Success
(Story from John Cohoat)

I was the chief executive officer of a hospital in the South Bend area, and the 40th anniversary of the facility was fast approaching. We decided the best way to celebrate was to find a memorable way to showcase our history.

I began by hiring a history professor from the local university. He examined some of the older files we had on site, and interviewed physicians who had worked there in the past, as well as their families. He found others who were there for the founding of the hospital and got as much of the story behind its beginnings as he could.

The end result was a 60-page history chronicling the hospital's story and how it had served the community successfully for the past four decades. We added some vintage and current pictures of the hospital as well, and made it into a nice little book that we published and gave to all the physicians and board members, as well as all the other employees and volunteers who worked at the hospital. It also came in handy as a giveaway at some community events.

Was this more than a vanity project? Yes, much more because it really focused everyone at the hospital on the original mission of the hospital, the reasons it was built and what it was all about. That brought a renewed sense of purpose and camaraderie to everyone who worked there.

And not only that, but it really impressed our patients. People take things like hospitals for granted. The book, however, brought it to life in a unique and entertaining way.

Recounting our history engaged and connected the whole staff, from top to bottom, and created a better work environment. And that meant a better experience for everyone - most importantly, our patients!

Your history can be an important asset to your business, if you find the right way to package it. It gives you more substance and more of a storyline that potential customers can respond to. People like stories. How did you start in business? What obstacles did you overcome?

Deliver Business Value
(Story from John Cohoat)

Back in 2010, I got together with a handful of entrepreneurs in my area and created a book that told the stories of 10 area companies. To get more impact from the publication of the book, I decided to create an event, and the date ended up falling around the first year anniversary of my local Glazer-Kennedy Insider Circle business growth chapter. It was natural to combine both milestones in one event, which I called "Celebrate Elkhart County Entrepreneurs." The event featured a guest speaker from out of town, as well as a panel discussion with all the authors of the book – and best of all, we made it free.

As all the featured entrepreneurs had extensive business experience, the audience members were able to ask them questions about how to get through tough times, their opinions of the current economy, what they thought were the keys to success, and other practical business advice from behind the closed boardroom doors.

The entrepreneurs were able to subtly showcase their own companies as well as demonstrate their business smarts to other business owners and local officials. – Meanwhile, the free event exceeded the attendees' expectations and provided a lot of useful information.

John Cohoat's Book,
"No Thank You, Mr., President"

I had asked the featured entrepreneurs to invite their own guests to hear them tell their story.

Nobody loses in an event such as this one.

Run a One-of-a-Kind Contest

(Story from John Cohoat)

The standard "fill-out-an-entry-and-you-might-win-blahblahblah..." kind of contest is pretty commonplace to the point where most people ignore them. But putting a different spin on this old standby can get you a lot more attention.

Our restaurant's variation was the "No Peeking" Contest that we'd do around Christmas time (but you could do this kind of thing anytime during the year).

We would take bright red envelopes and print a picture of a present on the front of them, along with the words, in big type, "No peeking!" Underneath, in smaller type, it would say, "Open this envelope the next time you come to see us and you'll win one of seven different prizes!" Now, the prize might be anything from a piece of pie or an appetizer to a $50 gift certificate or an overnight stay at a resort for two. We even had a grand prize of a 32-inch flat-screen TV.

We gave these envelopes to anyone who came to our restaurant during the entire month of December. It generated a lot of excitement because people knew they were eventually going to get *something*, guaranteed.

The real genius of the promotion was that customers had to come back during the month of January to redeem the envelope and claim their prizes. That's traditionally a very slow time of the year for us, so this helped increase our business when we needed the extra customers.

We held this contest for a few years in a row and it got to the point where, in October, people would already be asking if the "No Peeking" Contest was happening again. Along with the extra business, it gave us a higher profile and more public good will.

Eyes on the Prize

Anyone can offer cash as a door prize – everybody loves cash, right? But what does that do for the business offering the door prize? It isn't very memorable, in my experience, and what's the point of offering a prize that no one remembers?

That's why I prefer to choose a door prize that offers an experience of some kind. When someone gets a half day at the spa, or a round of golf for two, where they get to bring a friend, they're going to remember that fondly – and remember that you made it possible.

Even if you're running a contest just to generate some new leads, you'll find that you won't get as many people willing to give up their name and email for a $10 gift certificate as you would for an "experience" prize or something else that's different and attention-getting, like a test drive on a real racetrack or winning a chef for dinner.

Focus on one big prize instead of giving away a lot of little ones. Offer cool opportunities instead of everyday stuff. Be unique and memorable – not cheap and forgettable!

PART

12

Miscellaneous...
Life Lessons and
Other Stuff

Most of the tips in this book focus on specific marketing strategies. In this final section, we're going to look at overall ways you can change your brain to live a more profitable life. And we're not just talking about business – we're talking about your personal potential as well.

Sometimes we get stuck in patterns that prevent us from getting what we really want out of life. Rethinking those patterns and trying some new approaches can really open us up to all the possibilities that have been eluding us.

Master Your Mind

The person credited for coining the term *mastermind* is Napoleon Hill in his famous ground breaking book *Think and Grow Rich* which he wrote in the early 1900's. Mastermind groups, however, have actually been around as long as people have been around. You can even go back to the Bible and Jesus, constantly "masterminding" with his 12 disciples.

If you're not familiar with the concept, a mastermind group is where two or more people come together with a goal of helping each other. Each is able to access the others' strengths, which produces better results for all than any one of the people ever could possibly generate on their own.

You can create a mastermind group out of people in your own industry or, even better, from people outside your industry (all in non-competing businesses). I

I have local and national masterminds made up of up to 12 in the group

say "even better" because, when you're able to talk to business owners outside your industry, you're able to learn cool and fresh creative strategies that *no one else in your business sector is using.*

Sounds pretty good, huh?

I'd also be honored to have you join my Inner Circle Coaching MasterMind. Limited to just 10 business owners I have several groups.

1. Local business owners that meet once a month
2. Local CEO's / Presidents of company that also meet monthly
3. National Implementation mastermind. If you don't live close to northern Indiana, this would be the mastermind for you.

All the details can be found at **www.MegabucksMarketing.com/Coaching-Mastermind**

Live the Dream –
Before It's Reality!

It's important to remember where you ultimately want your business to take you (especially during a month when you may be struggling to make a mortgage payment). And a way to keep that inspiration of future success firmly implanted in your mind is to do the stuff now that you later hope to experience regularly later when you've found your path to prosperity.

· So go out there and test drive that Ferrari.

· Dress up and try that exclusive new restaurant.

· Peruse luxury travel magazines and plan your dream trip.

Yes, you have to live in the here and now, but your spirit should be set on earning the golden ticket to a better life. That makes you work harder and smarter toward your ultimate goals, which, in turn, helps you actually achieve them. This helps you to visualize your goals and keep them fresh in your mind. After all, you become what you think about.

Many people will tell you their favorite book for success thinking is "Think and Grow Rich" by Napoleon Hill.

I love that book also, but I was the most impacted by "Lazy Man's Way to Riches" by Joe Karbo. The original version is out of print but you may be lucky to find a used one on Amazon. There is a revised and expanded version, but my favorite is still the Karbo original.

Make Time for Pancakes
(Story from Dan Brekke)

This isn't directly about business or making money, but, to me, it's actually more important.

Every Wednesday morning I have a special breakfast with my boys.

SPECIAL BONUS TIP!!!!

For this breakfast, we've gone to the same pancake restaurant since they were born (for the most part). This quality time away from work gives me time to build a strong tradition with them, as well as a strong relationship.

These days, we're all so busy with our lives. We need to slow down and make time for our children, and this is one way I make time for them. I have it as a scheduled event on my calendar (as you should with any important personal goal) and I don't let anything else get in the way of it. Of course, on occasion, we have a hiccup. But we make it up on the weekend.

The point is this: As on-the-go entrepreneurs and salespeople, we often lose track of how fast our children grow so we need to set aside times like this to build a bond. After all, we're in business to give them (and us) the ultimate lifestyle. What good is that if we're all strangers at the end of the day?

And, to be honest, this kind of commitment also has a business-related benefit. You see, when you change the conversation with a potential buyer from I-sell-you-buy to "Here's what I do with my family, what do you do?" you set yourself apart and start a deeper personal relationship with the potential buyer...or should I say, your new friend! The next time you see that person, he or she is likely to immediately ask, "Well, how was the breakfast this week?"

It really creates a nice, strong relationship that fosters more work on the back end. The personal touch always pays off, whether it's with family or with business associates.

Dan with his two sons, Nathan and Grant

Appendix

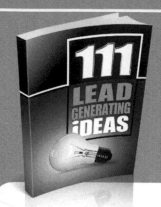

FREE

To receive this free special report, copy this page and FAX this form to 574-262-2314 or email to info@megabucksmarketing.com

The #1 question I get when I'm coaching clients is "How do I get More Customers?" It's a great question and one I've studied and tested lots of ideas in both my own business and my client's businesses. The problem is I'm a checklist kind of gal. It helps me focus, not forget anything, or simply jog my thinking.

But no such checklist existed that I could find for getting new customers.

So I created it.

I went through my files, my case studies, ideas from other bright marketers and put together a checklist of 111 Lead Generating ideas.

It's simple, but powerful and I'd like to give it to you for free as my way of saying "thank you" for reading my book.

This could very well become your most valuable marketing tool you have in your marketing toolbox.

All you have to do is fill out the following information and fax (574-262-2314) or email (info@megabucksmarketing.com) it back to me and I'll send it out right away to you.

Name _____

Business Name _____

Ship to Address _____

City, State Zip _____

Email _____

Work Phone _____

Website _____

Providing this information consistutes your permission for Megabucks Marketing to contact you regarding related information by mail, email, and phone

Newsletter
Template

Have you ever tried to produce a printed newsletter only to give up after a few short months?

Do you know you should be combining online AND offline to do multichannel marketing with a printed newsletter as a key component of your offline strategy, but don't know how?

Well, I have taken all the hassle of producing a printed newsletter from you.

ANNOUNCING THE MEGABUCKS MARKETING NEWSLETTER TEMPLATE

Each month you'll get a fully laid out newsletter template in Microsoft Publisher

All the content is included

It has my Star Cartoon as the newsletter mascot

It even includes my award winning humorous dog blog.

Details at

www.MegaBucksMarketing.com/ newsletter-templates

To Order Additional Copies of This Book

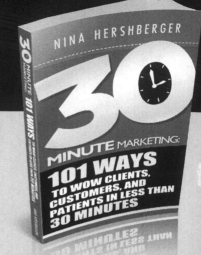

1	$19.95 *
2 – 10	$15.95 *
10 – 24	$12.95 *
25 – 100	$10.95 *
100 – 200	$9.95 *

Over 200 copies, call 574-320-2522 for quote

* Plus actual UPS Ground Shipping

☐ **AmEx** ☐ **Visa** ☐ **MC**

Card #

Exp date

Name on Card

Signature

Your Name (if different from above)

Business Name

Ship to Address

City, State Zip

Email

Work Phone

Website

Providing this information consistutes your permission for Megabucks Marketing to contact you regarding related information by mail, email, and phone

About the
Book Contributors

Though fellow Purdue University alumni may know him better as a Big 10 football player, **Dan Brekke** is now almost as famous as co-owner (with his wife)of Indiana Micro Metal Etching, a precision manufacturer of metal parts, Never one to let any grass grow under his feet, this long-time serial entrepreneur is also a commercial real estate developer who owns five mini storage locations with over 1,000 units.

"Once the processes are streamlined and automated, it's all about marketing," Dan explains. Dan and Leanne have two kids and run their worldwide manufacturing process out of Elkhart, Indiana.

Contact information: Dan@IndyMetalEtching.com

John Cannon uses outrageous marketing to attract new customers to Cannon's Automotive, an eight-bay auto repair shop in LaPorte, Indiana. But the real success of this small-town shop is in the day-to-day attention to detail that is the hallmark of John's 40 years in business. It's what keeps his customers coming back year-after-year, generation-after-generation.

After his military tour, John returned home to Indiana and cleaned out his entire life savings to purchase a run-down gas station. With the help of his brother, a lot of elbow grease, and some badly needed new equipment, Cannon's Automotive was in business. Long after most shops would have closed, Cannon's is a thriving business in this small Indiana town.

Contact information: john.cannonsauto@frontier.com

John Cohoat has been a serial entrepreneur and executive in the Northern Indiana area for over 30 years. He has owned several successful companies including Bonnie Doone Ice Cream and The Patchwork Quilt Country Inn. Throughout his career, John has been masterfully skilled in the strategic planning of business operations, which has been instrumental in the growth of his companies.

Recently John took the opportunity to become the Northern Indiana and SW Michigan Local Certified No BS Business Growth Advisor in affiliation with Glazer-Kennedy Insider's Circle. John has received extensive training by both Dan Kennedy and Bill Glazer and is in constant communication with GKIC headquarters, receiving advance notice of meetings, new tools, seminars, and information products that are made available to local chapter members.

Contact information: john@cohoatbusinessgrowth.com

Jamahl Keyes is widely recognized all over the world as the "Magic Motivator" – a leading expert in helping people reach their full potential in whatever they choose to do in life. As a motivator and coach, Jamahl has developed a variety of presentations to help people hand people the *Keyes 2 Success*, from those just getting started to people who need help redirecting their already established lives.

A top-selling author of four books

- *Can't Quit It:Leadership and Success Strategies*
- *101 Ways to Brand Yourself: How to Stand Out in the Corporate World*
- *Student Success Stories: Goal Setting and Adversity Strategies*
- *Marketing Machine: How to Market Your Business Online and Offline*

"The Magic Motivator" Jamahl Keyes has helped 100's of students position themselves in the competitive and challenging corporate world and has also helped small business owners market their product and/or service to millions. He has helped prevent headaches of figuring out the next step not only in business but in life giving people easy to implement strategies to help them grow. He has also helped millions of college students step out into the corporate world to catch or create their dream job and giving them points of instructions on how to stand out from the rest of any other applicants.

Contact information: jamahl@jamahlkeyes.com

Growing up the youngest of 11 children, **Bert Molner** wasn't exactly born with a silver spoon in his mouth. But instead of whining about hand-me-down clothes and gently-used toys, he did something about it, starting his own leather craft business at the age of 13. Apparently, he had a knack for it – by the age of 16, he had earned his own Dunn & Bradstreet rating! And since then, he has never looked back. After putting himself through Michigan State University with his earnings, he leapt leaped immediately into the notoriously difficult housing industry, with 12 job offers. achievingHe attained huge success with both America's largest housing company and the world's largest housing project.

From there, it was on to the financial sector, but Bert didn't exactly launch his financial career in the traditional way. His own financial advisor was so impressed with Bert's investment savvy that he insisted he join the firm. Three years later, Bert was ranked number one in the world for new firm growth – out of a field of over 10,000 financial advisors!

Passionate about creating financial opportunity for all, Bert has served as president of his county's estate planning council, founded the Bristol Business Network and served on the legislative committee with Indiana State Treasurer Richard Mourdock. Today, he is pursuing a new dream, hoping to use his vast and impressive financial knowledge to lead a company as a CEO.

Passionate about creating financial opportunity for all, Bert has served as president of his county's estate planning council, founded the Bristol Business Network and served on the

legislative committee with Indiana State Treasurer Richard Mourdock.   Today, he is pursuing a new dream, hoping to use his vast and impressive financial knowledge to lead a company as a CEO.

Contact Information: financial.x.bert@gmail.com

If you know anything about the auction business in the Midwest, you probably know the name **Willis Yoder**. He's a highly-skilled auctioneer – the Michigan state champion as well as two-time International Auctioneer finalist – and the creative force behind several products that are highly sought-after in the auction arena.

After moving to Indiana from Michigan, Willis launched a -successful business manufacturing auction trailers, which he sold a few years ago. More recently, he designed the industry's first portable auction podium and just released a more compact collapsible model.

In addition to his manufacturing business, Willis continues to work as an auctioneer and organizes major auctions and trade shows in Northern Indiana to promote local craftsman and small businesses. When he's not helping clients turn their assets and estates into cash, he enjoys raising pure-bred Labrador dogs and is an avid hunter, gun collector, and outdoorsman.

Contact Information: premierrehabhomes@yahoo.com